Sharing the Good New
A Workbook on Personal Evangelism

James R. Driscoll

James R. Driscoll, Publisher

Delia,
what a joy to meet you
and to share together at this
Making Disciples Weekend!
I am thrilled with our
"Lemmon SD" connections!
God bless,
Jim Driscoll

SHARING THE GOOD NEWS:
A WORKBOOK ON PERSONAL EVANGELISM

FIRST EDITION
Copyright 1997 by
James R. Driscoll

ISBN 0-7880-0967-2

PRINTED IN U.S.A.

To Katheryn, Rebecca, and Michael:
you are signs of God's Good News in my life

ACKNOWLEDGMENTS

I wish to thank Dr. James Logan at Wesley Theological Seminary for his support and encouragement in the development of this workbook. His contributions through Wesley Seminary's Doctor of Ministry in Evangelism program were formative for my thinking and practice of evangelism.

I am also very grateful to the people of Harmony United Methodist Church in Hamilton, Virginia, for their interest and support. The Harmony congregation has been the laboratory in which this workbook was developed.

Finally, I could not have produced this book without the support of my wife, Katheryn, and my parents, Jim and Shirley Driscoll, in Connellsville, Pennsylvania.

CONTENTS

INTRODUCTION

Evangelism is a key aspect of our lives as Christians. For some years, many Christians have tended to avoid any serious practice or study of evangelism. Perhaps we were unsure how to do it. Perhaps we got caught up in other aspects of the Christian life. Perhaps we had seen models of evangelism that offended us or turned us off, so we steered clear of evangelism. Whatever the case, for a lot of years, evangelism has been out of vogue in much of the mainline Christian community.

In recent years, there has been a resurgence of interest in evangelism. Some of this interest has been channeled into the church growth movement. Training and seminars abound on how to grow the church. Mega-churches have popped up at various places around the country, and church leaders are flocking to them to see how they do it. While I do not reject the teachings of church growth and believe that much of their methods are practical and helpful, church growth is not all there is to evangelism. While effective evangelism may result in church growth, and it is hoped will result in church growth, evangelism is about more than church growth.

In essence, evangelism is about all that the church does. When Jesus is named, evangelism can include everything from proclaiming the good news, to bringing new disciples into the community we call the church, to practicing outreach and working for social change. Evangelism is a broad-based discipline that is at the root of all we do as the church.

This study will look at one part of evangelism, the practice of personally talking about Jesus Christ and sharing the good news. I believe that this is an area we often overlook in mainline churches. We are not sure how to talk about our faith in a way that is tasteful and graceful. We do not want to offend or step on toes. We do not want to appear to be religious fanatics, so, in response, we avoid personal encounters where we share the gospel message. We know that it is something we should do. We want to be able to do it. But instead, we keep the good news we know and have experienced to ourselves. Naturally this is not the norm for everyone, but it is true of many mainline Christians.

This six-week study is designed to address our need and desire to share our faith. Over the course of these six weeks I will present theoretical and practical materials that will, it is hoped, help each student feel better equipped to share his or her understanding of the good news. The idea is not to make us all street preachers who will tally up hundreds of converts. Instead, I hope that those of you taking part in this study will simply be better prepared and able to talk about Jesus with your family, with your friends, with your coworkers, and with persons you may encounter as you live out your life from day to day.

THE PLAN

This study will take six weeks and has two major components. First, study participants will meet weekly for approximately one and one-half hours. The weekly meetings will include opportunities for prayer, discussion, and input from the leader. Some of the focus of the meeting will be the material covered in the study guide during the previous week. Some sessions may include activities, role plays, or exercises. Please do not let these experiential learning activities frighten you. I believe that by practicing sharing the good news in a safe environment where we are friends, we will be more comfortable sharing the good news in the places we find ourselves everyday. Some of the sessions may also include tasks to be completed during the coming week. Examples of these might be visiting with shut-ins or prospective church members. The study sessions should be fun, enlightening, and lively.

The second major component of the six weeks is the study guide. This guide has been designed to be used every day during the six weeks. Please make a commitment to spend a period of time, preferably **twenty to thirty** minutes per day working in the book. **Do not put it all off until the last day of the week.** The study is designed so that each day's reading and work build on the previous day and should be the focus of the day for which it is assigned. Naturally, you will occasionally miss a day and need to make up two days at once. This is understandable and okay. But please, make every attempt to set aside some time each day to work on the assignment for the day and then think about it, reflect on it, and pray about it until you begin the next day's material. This study will be most effective if you work on it one day at a time as it has been designed.

Each day is divided into three parts. The first part is some material to read, reflect on, and digest. Do not read this hurriedly, but slowly and thoughtfully. Take notes in the margins, underline, and jot down questions you want to discuss when the full group gathers. Some of the ideas presented may be new to you. You may not always agree with what is presented. I invite you to read the material and interact with it as you work on each day of the study.

The second section of the day is called **"Think About It."** This portion of the material usually includes questions and invites a response. Take some time as you work to answer the question or do the suggested activity. If you cannot answer at that moment, carry the question in your mind for a while and come back to it later. The "Think About It" section is your chance to reflect on the material and make it your own.

The third section of each day is called **"Try It Out."** The "Try It Out" section will usually invite you to do an exercise or some kind of activity during the day. Some of these will be very easy. Some may be more challenging and you may find that you resist the suggested activity. Please make your best attempt to do the activity suggested in this section. Our efforts to put our learnings into action will help us better reach the goal of this study: sharing the good news of Jesus Christ.

A NOTE TO THE LEADER

Each weekly session includes a guide to be followed during the group meeting for the week. The group meeting breaks down into several basic parts following this basic outline:

Praying together

Praying together is the opportunity to share joys and concerns together as a group. This will probably take more than a traditional thirty-second opening prayer. My experience is that taking time to share and pray seriously binds the group together and makes for a more powerful, meaningful group experience. I suggest that five to ten minutes be set aside for this time of sharing and prayer. Group members may want to pray for this study, experiences they are having as they attempt to share good news, and successful encounters they have had in sharing good news.

Review of this week's material

This is the opportunity to explore the material the group members covered during their individual study sessions during the past week. You may choose to go through day by day, to look at the "Think About It" sections for each day, or to ask what was most meaningful or most difficult. This may also be an opportunity to discuss their experiences in the "Try It Out" section. Reserve thirty to forty minutes for this sharing.

Exercises, role plays, or case studies

Some weeks the session will suggest ideas for exercises, role plays, or case studies. Use these as you see fit. You may want to use one idea or you may want to use them all. Perhaps you can divide a larger group into two or three sub-groups to do their own exercise. The smaller groups could then report back to the larger group or present their role play or experience. I encourage you to use these when they are suggested. They will provide a safe way to experience sharing the gospel in a controlled environment. By practicing in the group setting, persons will be better prepared to share good news in other settings. Twenty minutes is probably a good time frame for this activity.

Telling our story

Telling our story is the opportunity for one or two members of the group to share their testimony with the rest of the group. While the idea of telling our stories is developed in detail during week four, it may be helpful to encourage persons to begin thinking about their own faith stories before that session. By practicing and hearing one another's stories, the group will be better equipped to tell faith stories to persons outside the group.

Leader Input

Each week offers a section called leader input. This is material that the leader can present to the group to supplement the material that is offered during the week. It can be presented in lecture format or the group can read it together. It can be simply presented, or it can be the starting point for a discussion. Some of the leader input sections prepare the way for the coming week's session while others are designed to complement what has been presented during the previous week. This can probably be done in five to ten minutes.

Assignments

This study is an experiential exercise. It is hoped that as persons experience sharing the good news themselves, they will be more and more at ease, and faith sharing will become a regular part of everyday life. Thus, assignments will be suggested each week to be done before the next session. These assignments are done in addition to the daily "Try It Out" sections and can be done as individuals or in small groups.

Visits to prospects, shut-ins

The leader may wish to give group members the opportunity to build relationships and develop interpersonal faith-sharing skills by inviting them to visit with prospective members, shut-ins, or inactive members. This is not a requirement to complete the course, but can be a helpful way to develop skills while benefiting the church and those who receive visits.

Telling our story next week

This portion of the session is simply the opportunity to solicit volunteers who will be prepared to share their testimony at next week's group meeting.

Testimonies at worship

Some members of the group may wish to offer a testimony by telling their story at worship. Each week, invite persons to tell their story at worship, and then arrange for the pastor to include them in the upcoming Sunday morning worship service. These testimonies can be brief (three to five minutes) and again provide a safe way to rehearse the process of thinking about and telling one's own faith story.

Closing prayer time

The closing prayer time is a time to pray together as a group and conclude the session. Find creative ways to do this. Sing a song, share a prayer in unison, join hands, share in communion, or gather around a cross and candles. One highly effective idea is to have each person place his or her name and telephone number on a three by five card. At the end of the session, pair off the cards. These pairs will be prayer partners during the coming week. Give the pairs five minutes to meet together and pray with each other before officially closing the session. Ask that prayer partners call or visit each other during the week to pray, talk, and encourage one another as they discuss their learnings from the week's material.

Evaluation

After the official session is concluded, I suggest that the leader take a few minutes for objective evaluation. Ask three questions:

> What went well?
> What did not go well?
> What changes would you make?

Newsprint may be used for recording the group's answers.

YOUR OWN PREPARATION FOR EVANGELISM

You and I are best prepared to share good news and talk about Jesus when our own spiritual lives are alive and disciplined. When we are working on our own faith, when it is vital and being nourished and exercised, we are better prepared to do this important work that our Lord calls us to do.

What are the elements of a healthy, growing spiritual life? The best model I have been introduced to is a historical model developed by the founder of the Methodist movement, John Wesley. John Wesley called Christians to a discipleship that exercised the spirit, nurtured the faith, and brought Christians into accountable relationships with one another.

This accountable discipleship is best expressed by the General Rule of Discipleship, which is: "To witness to Jesus Christ in the world and to follow his teachings through acts of compassion, justice, worship, and devotion under the guidance of the Holy Spirit."

This model of discipleship presents a balanced approach to the Christian life. A person who is embarking on a life of discipleship will focus on living out his or her Christianity in the four areas named in the General Rule of Discipleship. They are:

- **Compassion**-Feeding the hungry, caring for the sick, healing those who hurt, and generally showing compassion.
- **Justice**-Working for justice in the world to make the world more like the Kingdom of God.
- **Devotion**-Your own personal life of prayer, scripture study, and reflection.
- **Worship**-Participation in a life of worship that includes partaking of the Sacraments and listening to God's word.

A living, growing spiritual life includes these four aspects. As you embark on this study, I invite you to look at your own spiritual life. Are there areas that are emphasized more than others? Are there areas you are neglecting completely? Use these six weeks as an opportunity to develop your own spiritual life. Make a commitment to this during this time. A healthy, growing spiritual life is essential to effective sharing of good news.

13

GETTING STARTED

Now you begin your six week journey. We will start with a session that will introduce the study and give an overview of what lies ahead. Have fun, try out some of the suggestions that are offered, and experience the fulfillment that comes from sharing the GOOD NEWS God offers to us in Jesus Christ.

INTRODUCTORY GROUP MEETING

Praying together

Overview of the course

Discuss the Introduction

Leader Input

Each of the four Gospels has its own version of the great commission. I have included comments that can be shared as reflection on the great commission as it appears in John's Gospel. The group should read this passage from John 20 at this time. The other passages will be read and discussed at various points throughout the course. The four great commissions are:

Matthew 28:16-20
Mark 16:14-20
Luke 24:44-49
John 20:19-23

John's Great Commission: Incarnational Evangelism

The disciples were scared to death. Jesus had been killed and they didn't know what to do. They were hiding, the doors locked tight. If they were caught, their fate might be the same as his.

He had been put to death on Friday. Here it was Sunday evening. As they met behind those closed doors, Jesus appeared. Their Lord had risen. It was he. He showed them his side and his hands. They could touch the places where the nails had been driven. Suddenly, it wasn't so scary anymore.

And then he spoke. "Peace be with you. As the father has sent me, so I send you" (John 20:21, NRSV). There it is, John's version of the Great Commission.

Jesus is calling his disciples, and you and me, to get out from behind our locked doors, to get up from our pews, to move out of our beautiful sanctuaries...and be about his work. "As the Father has sent me, so I send you."

Jesus is challenging us to be involved in what is called incarnational evangelism. To incarnate means to make real. Jesus calls his disciples to do evangelism that makes the good news real.

Let me give an example. Our church has some excellent teachers in our Sunday School. One of those is Sharon Myers. One Sunday, my daughter Rebecca came home and I asked her what she had learned in Sunday School. She proceeded to tell me about how Mrs. Myers had set up a make-believe well in the classroom. She played the part of the troubled woman at the well while her sister, Mrs. Wilson, played the part of Jesus and they acted out the story for those children. And the children remembered the story.

That is incarnation. Incarnation takes something beyond being a concept and makes it something you can touch, hold, feel, experience, and understand.

Jesus incarnated God. He came to earth to make God real, among God's people. God sent him to show first hand what God is like. In Jesus, God was no longer a concept. He was a real man with flesh and blood.

Now Jesus says, "Just as God sent me, now I am sending you. Just as God sent me to incarnate him, I am sending you to incarnate my message, my love, and my grace." That is incarnational evangelism.

Incarnational evangelism is the conscious effort to make the unconditional love of Jesus real and alive in every place you go and in every relationship you have. That means that you don't need to look for special, out of the ordinary opportunities to do evangelism. You can evangelize every moment of every day. You can evangelize with or without words. You can evangelize as you do the acts that make Jesus real and incarnate his grace and his teachings in your home, in your workplace, and in your community.

Assignments
> **Visits to prospects, shut-ins**
> **Telling our story next week**
> **Testimonies at worship**

Closing Prayer Time

Evaluation

WHY TALK ABOUT JESUS?

DAY ONE: *Evangelism: A Frightening Word*

Evangelism.

Few words in the Christian vocabulary carry so much baggage. Few words conjure such mixed images. We hear the word and immediately think about television preachers, tent meetings, and young men in white shirts knocking at our doors. We think about being put on the spot by enthusiastic followers of Jesus who want to know: "If you die tonight, are you going to heaven?" We remember times our privacy has been breached by those who inquire about the innermost things of the spirit without even knowing us or really caring about us. We think of pamphlets thrust into our hands on sidewalks, at malls, at airports, or in the center of town.

And we think, "That's not for me."

"That's not my style."

"That's not my kind of religion. If it has to do with evangelism, leave me out of it."

Such reactions are not uncommon. Such reactions are valid.

The downside is that in our efforts to avoid the negative side of evangelism as we have experienced it in the past, we end up avoiding evangelism all together. Instead of merely steering clear from the pressure tactics others have used when talking about Jesus, we end up not talking about Jesus at all.

And that makes us feel guilty. Christians are supposed to talk about Jesus, aren't they? We Christians claim that Jesus makes a difference in our lives. We claim that he is the reference point about which we center our values, priorities, and morals. We believe that Jesus somehow makes a change in who we are, that he is the giver of eternal life, that he provides strength in the midst of the storm. But maybe we don't feel comfortable talking about him that much.

We don't want to offend.

We don't want to take advantage of our friendships.

We don't want people to think we are fanatics.   So we end up not talking about Jesus.

And we feel guilty.

The purpose of this study is to spend six weeks thinking about that part of Christian life we call evangelism. We will look at what it means to evangelize. We will think about why we avoid opportunities to talk about Jesus. We will examine some tools for talking about Jesus and even practice a little bit.

Our hope is that at the end of our time together, we will all feel better equipped to talk about the one who is the center and Savior of our life. We will find ways to share without being afraid or being ashamed. We will find ways to talk about Jesus gracefully out of our deep care and concern for our world and those around us.

And we may even discover some new things about evangelism. Perhaps evangelism is even more than talking about Jesus....

THINK ABOUT IT
What is your reaction when you think about evangelism?

Can you identify with any of the reactions noted above?

Do you feel guilty about not talking more about your faith in Jesus Christ?

TRY IT OUT
Spend some time over the next couple of days talking with family members, friends, and other members of your church. How do they feel about evangelism? How do they respond to that word? Do they talk about Jesus with others?

DAY TWO: *A Little Good News*

I live in Loudoun County, Virginia, about thirty miles west of Washington, D.C. Our local television stations are the stations based in Washington. One of those is WTTG Channel 5, the local Fox affiliate. Channel 5 is the only station that offers a news program at 10:00 p.m. All of the others offer news at 11:00 p.m. Many nights, my wife and I don't want to stay up until 11:00 to catch the headlines, so we tune in at 10:00 to learn what is going on.

Most nights we wish we hadn't.

The first fifteen to twenty minutes of every newscast seem to be focused on killings, rapes, muggings, and accidents. Every night, the news seems a little worse than it was the night before. We want to get the news but for the most part, the news seems to be nothing but bad news.

Is there any good news?

Who wants bad news at 10:00 p.m.? Here we are ready to relax, ready to sleep, ready to unwind. However, by the time we watch the 10 o'clock news for a few minutes, our pulses are up, our blood pressures are elevated, and we are edgy, uptight, and anxious. When we really want to sleep, we skip the news with all of its violence and tragedy, and go read a good book. (Unfortunately, this means we miss the weather report; it doesn't come on until after all the bad news has been broadcast.)

Some years back, Ann Murray recorded a country western song that calls for "A Little Good News." She sings, "We sure could use a little good news today."[1] I, for one, can certainly relate.

All around us is a world that is crying out for good news.

We who are Christians bring good news to this troubled, bad news world. When we engage in evangelism, we engage in "good newsing" the world in which we live.

The primary word for evangelism is the Greek noun, *euangelion*. This Greek word basically means "good message" or "good news." Thus, to evangelize is to spread good news. This good news is, of course, the good news of the Kingdom of God. Evangelism is the process of communicating the good news of what God has done in Jesus Christ. It is the announcement of hope that comes through God's coming to this world in human

---

[1]"A Little Good News," (Tommy Rocco, Rory Michael Bourke), 1983, Bibo Music Publishers, Inc., Charlie Black; Welk Music & Chappell & Co.

form, dying on a cross, and rising from the grave to bring forgiveness of sins and eternal life in the face of the darkness of death.

The world needs a little good news. Fortunately, when Christians are around, there is an ever present source of good news...God's good news. And that is the best news of all.

THINK ABOUT IT
How do you experience the gospel of Jesus Christ as good news?

Is the concept of evangelism as sharing good news a new concept to you?

Think of a time you had good news to share. Write a little about it in this space.

Did you tell others your good news? How did you feel as you shared your good news? Is sharing the good news of the gospel really any different?

TRY IT OUT
Continue with the informal survey and discussions you began yesterday. It might be interesting to ask if your friends and family experience evangelism as good news.

DAY THREE: *The Good News: Abundant Life*

Today we continue to think about evangelism as a process of sharing good news. As we have seen, the basis of evangelism is God's good news as demonstrated through Jesus Christ. In short, evangelism is the process of bringing persons and the world at large into contact with the good news of Jesus Christ in hopes that the good news will challenge, change, transform, and make whole those with whom it is shared.

The Bible speaks about the good news of Jesus Christ in numerous places. However, one verse stands out as a key verse in understanding the good news, the purpose of Jesus' life, and the meaning of evangelism. In John 10:10, Jesus said, "I came that they may have life, and have it abundantly" (NRSV). These words are at the center of evangelism. To evangelize is to bring life to those persons and places which are dead, and to bring it in abundance. Bringing life, wholeness, reconciliation, and restoration is central to what Jesus was about and is central to what we are about as Christians and evangelists. The source of this abundant life is the good news that God has acted to redeem this broken world. That redemption has been effected in Jesus Christ and will be completed at the time of his return.

Announcing good news and bringing abundant life may be a new concept of evangelism to you.

I find this understanding of evangelism to be very freeing. I find this understanding of evangelism to be refreshing.

This concept of evangelism frees it from many of our preconceived notions that burden much of our thinking about evangelism. Evangelism cannot be reduced to a four-step process that leads to salvation. Evangelism cannot be reduced to the process of making Christians. Evangelism cannot be judged as successful or unsuccessful by counting up the number of faith commitments one has been instrumental in receiving, as though it were kind of like closing a successful sale or deal. Evangelism is an ongoing process that takes place both outside the walls of the church as well as within the church itself. Evangelism happens each time the good news of Jesus Christ is shared, both in words and actions, with the intent of bringing life with abundance. Thus evangelism is at the heart of the ministry and life of the church. The church is in the business of bringing the source of abundant life to those places where life is being diminished. The church is in the business of evangelism.

THINK ABOUT IT
Is your understanding of evangelism growing or getting broader? How?

If evangelism is really offering life in abundance, what are some activities you or your church or your family engage in that are evangelistic?

As we engage in these activities that bring abundant life, is it important or even necessary to mention the fact that we do these life-giving acts in, through, or because of Jesus Christ? Why or why not?

TRY IT OUT

Continue to discuss evangelism with your family and friends. Introduce some of your new concepts and understandings to them. How do they react?

DAY FOUR: *More Than Making Converts*

So far we have talked about evangelism as a process of offering good news. We share the good news of Jesus Christ in a world that has more than its share of bad news. We have also equated evangelism with offering abundant life. As Christian disciples and evangelists, we offer abundant life, forgiveness, reconciliation, and wholeness to people and places that are lifeless and broken.

So far we have said little about making converts. Isn't that the goal of evangelism? To make more Christians? To make more people who think as we do? To get people saved? Isn't that why we are supposed to evangelize and talk about Jesus? Don't we want to have a winning score? Isn't our goal to get as many souls as we can recorded on that divine master list God keeps somewhere in heaven?

Listen to what Eddie Fox and George Morris say about evangelism's concern for making converts: "Let us be clear that the constituent element in evangelization is the good news of the kingdom of God. Therefore, evangelization is never present unless the good news of the kingdom of God is present. Fundamentally, evangelism is an ongoing process of communication involving this gospel."[2]

Perhaps this is a new definition of evangelism for you. Quite often we make the mistake of defining evangelism as the process of making converts. We believe that if we are truly engaging in evangelism, we are telling others about Christ and converting them so that they become followers. According to this way of thinking, the responsibility for successful evangelism is ours. The outcome is based on how effectively we convince others of the gospel truth. We are successful if they are converted. If they do not respond in faith, we have failed.

This kind of understanding of evangelism fails to recognize one key truth: It is God who converts. It is not up to you or me to get someone to convert. The converting of the heart is God's action, God's doing. You and I are responsible simply to evangelize and that means announcing and spreading the good news of the Kingdom.

Our desire ultimately is that conversion will happen. We hope and pray that those who hear the gospel will commit their lives to Christ and become Christians. But

---

[2]H. Eddie Fox and George Morris Faith Sharing (Nashville: Discipleship Resources, 1986), 43.

evangelism in its most basic sense is the spread of the good news, regardless of the results.

Perhaps this definition is different from your previous understanding of evangelism. Perhaps it is even difficult to hear. You and I live in a success-oriented culture. Everything we do, whether in business, or sports, or academics, or other pursuits, seems to be measured, evaluated, and compared. We want to be successful. We are expected to be successful. If we have not achieved measurable results, we must have failed somehow or somewhere.

Successful evangelism, however, doesn't mean success in gaining numbers of converts. Successful evangelism faithfully spreads the word, announces the truth, shares the gospel and then recognizes that, ultimately, the results are in God's hands.

Isn't this a liberating concept?

It means you don't have to fret over the results. You don't need to feel you have failed when you have not achieved any converts. Some people shy away from evangelism because they fear this kind of failure. Yet, when it comes to evangelizing, the only failure is failure to faithfully spread the good news. You can be free, liberated from anxiety and worry over the results!

This concept of evangelism is quite biblical. Jesus himself advocated a style of evangelism that broadcast the good news while leaving the results up to God when he told the parable of the sower in Matthew 13:3-9 (NRSV):

> Listen! A sower went out to sow. And as he sowed, some seeds fell on the path, and the birds came and ate them up. Other seeds fell on rocky ground, where they did not have much soil, and they sprang up quickly, since they had no depth of soil. But when the sun rose, they were scorched; and since they had no root, they withered away. Other seeds fell among thorns, and the thorns grew up and choked them. Other seeds fell on good soil and brought forth grain, some a hundredfold, some sixty, some thirty. Let anyone with ears, listen!

Eddie Fox and George Morris seem to have the story of the sower in mind when they write, "Evangelization is defined as spreading the gospel of the kingdom of God by word and deed and then waiting in respectful humility and working with expectant hope."[3]

THINK ABOUT IT

It is God who converts. Our job is to share the good news. How does that idea make you feel about being involved in evangelism?

Is this a new concept of evangelism for you? Is evangelism any less frightening or intimidating for you?

TRY IT OUT

Consider the discussions you have had this week about evangelism. How do you and others respond to evangelism when it doesn't require the need to "close the deal," "make the sale," or "win the convert?"

DAY FIVE: *What Is Your Motive?*

Joe Donaho tells the story of the time he met an elderly man in the Atlanta airport. The man had a large sign hanging around his neck which read, "For whosoever shall call upon the name of the Lord shall be saved" (Romans 10:13, KJV). Donaho was intrigued by this novel approach to evangelism and stopped to talk to the gentleman. The man said that he had been in the airport for 1,000 hours over a two-year period. As Donaho went on his way, the man gave him a card which read, "By the help of the Lord, I am trying to keep people out of hell!"[4] The man in the airport had a pretty clear motivation for his involvement in his style of evangelism.

Christians have engaged in evangelism and faith sharing for varieties of reasons in the past as well as the present. Some of those motivations are more legitimate than others. A list of motivations for evangelism might include:

- To make our church grow.
- To preserve our denomination.
- To preserve souls from eternal torment in Hell.

---

[3]Ibid., 44.
[4]Joe Donaho, Good News Travels Faster (Decatur, Georgia: CTS Press, 1990), 43.

- To raise money for a dwindling budget.
- A sense of duty calls on us to evangelize.
- Love and concern for our world, our society, and our fellow human beings.
- A sense of guilt.
- The witness of the Bible.
- A sense of gratitude to God for the grace and love we receive in Jesus Christ.
- Loyalty to our church and its programs.
- A desire to get as many as possible converted and saved.
- The redemption of society.
- A response to the Great Commission in which Christ calls us to make disciples.
- To share good news and abundant life with our world and others.
- Fear of God's wrath.
- To gain God's approval.

THINK ABOUT IT

What motivations would you add to the list above?

Which are poor motivations for doing evangelism? Why?

Which are more appropriate, appealing reasons for doing evangelism? Why?

How does your motivation affect the way you do evangelism?

TRY IT OUT

Try to take note throughout the day of what motivates people. What motivates the telemarketer, what motivates the people you work with, what motivates the salespersons you encounter? Consider how or if Christian motivations for evangelism are any different.

DAY SIX: *Some Biblical Evangelists*

Perhaps the best place to look for examples of evangelism is in the pages of the Bible. We find there varieties of styles and methods for sharing the good news that is the gospel. Take a few moments today to look at these models of evangelism.

Andrew

Andrew was an inviter. Each time we see him in the scriptures, he is introducing people to Jesus. Andrew was concerned about helping others make connections with the Messiah.

The first time we see Andrew is at the beginning of John's Gospel. In John 1:40-43 (NRSV), we read, "One of the two who heard John speak was Andrew, Simon Peter's brother. He first found his brother Simon and said to him, 'We have found the Messiah.' He brought Simon to Jesus..." If it had not been for Andrew's introduction, Peter would not have been in a position to become Jesus' key disciple and the foundation for the Christian Church.

A little later in Jesus' ministry, a large crowd of people have gathered to hear Jesus; they are very hungry. John tells us that it was Andrew who introduced Jesus and the little boy with five loaves and two fish (John 6:8-9). Later we find some Greeks wanting to meet Jesus. They came to Philip with their request. Naturally, Philip went to Andrew and Andrew went and told Jesus (John 12:22).

Andrew arranged for people to meet Jesus. He invited them to meet his beloved Master.

Philip

Philip gives us an example of evangelism by listening, asking appropriate questions, and using an appropriate sense of timing. Acts 8:26-39 tells of Philip's interaction with the Ethiopian eunuch. Prompted by the Lord, Philip goes to the chariot where the eunuch is seated. Philip doesn't begin to preach or teach. He simply begins a conversation and invites dialogue by asking, "Do you understand what you are reading?" The eunuch, reading from Isaiah, indicates that he does not. He invites Philip to sit with him and he asks Philip for more information. With patience and gentleness, Philip "proclaimed to him the good news about Jesus." Timing, an invitational style, appropriate questions, and an ability to listen marked Philip's evangelistic style.

Barnabas

Barnabas' name means "Son of Encouragement." And encouragement is just what Barnabas excelled at. In Acts 4:36-37 he sells his property and gives the proceeds to the church. In Acts 9:26-27, he offers encouragement to Paul. Again in Acts 11:25,

Barnabas encourages Paul. In Acts 15:12 we see Barnabas welcoming Gentiles into the fellowship. Later in verses 36-39 he speaks up on behalf of John Mark and offers him support and encouragement.

Barnabas is willing to speak up, to help those who are often overlooked or left out. He stands by one engaged in controversy. These are ways of conveying good news. These are models for doing evangelism. Barnabas gives us the example of evangelism by encouragement.

These examples from the Bible make it clear that there is no one way to do evangelism. Andrew, Philip, and Barnabas each had distinct styles. Yet each one was engaged in sharing good news and promoting abundant life.

It is hoped that, looking at these biblical models will help you realize that there is no one way to evangelize, no one way you have to talk about Jesus. And that can be very freeing.

THINK ABOUT IT
Can you think of other biblical models for evangelism?

What appeals to you in each of these models?
Andrew:

Philip:

Barnabas:

TRY IT OUT
Select one of the three models we introduced today: Andrew who invited, Philip who listened and gently asked questions, or Barnabas who offered encouragement. Think about the model you chose and look for an opportunity to put your model into practice. Offer an invitation, listen and gently question, or give someone your encouragement.

DAY SEVEN: *Witnesses for Jesus*

The story of Jesus' ascension is recorded in Acts 1:6-9 (NRSV):

> So when they had come together, they asked him, "Lord, is this the
> time when you will restore the kingdom to Israel?" He replied, "It is
> not for you to know the times or periods that the Father has set by
> his own authority. But you will receive power when the Holy Spirit
> has come upon you; and you will be my witnesses in Jerusalem, in all
> Judea, and Samaria, and to the ends of the earth." When he had said
> this, as they were watching he was lifted up, and a cloud took him
> out of their sight.

Jesus' call to his disciples and to you and to me in this passage is very clear. He calls us to
be witnesses. In other words, he calls on his followers to be evangelists. He wants us to
offer testimony to the good news. We are to advertise it. We are to tell what we know.
We are to share that which offers abundant life. We are to witness.

Most of us are pretty clear about what it is that witnesses do. They tell what they know.
They tell what they have seen. As I write this, the trial of O.J. Simpson has just concluded.
For over a year, we have been subjected to countless reports about the progress of the
trial. Every evening newscast told of the witness who appeared that day. The witnesses
each gave their perspectives on what had happened. They shared what they had heard,
seen, or knew.

Interestingly enough, the witnesses didn't control the outcome of the trial. That was up to
someone else. That was up to the jury. But the witnesses had an important, essential role
in getting the information out.

In much the same way, you and I are witnesses. We tell and share what we know and
have experienced. We tell of this man of Nazareth who lived and died and rose. We
witness to our faith which gives strength, and assures us of forgiveness, and offers a moral
rudder for this life. We testify about what we believe to be the truth of an eternal life in
God's Kingdom. We are witnesses.

We do not control the outcome. We do not force our hearers to decide one way or the
other. Some who hear may respond in faith. Some may respond in disbelief. Some may
hear our witness, only to remember it years later and come to faith at another time in their
life.

In any case, Jesus calls us to witness. That is the task of evangelism.

Jesus also tells where to witness. He says to start with Jerusalem. In other words, start at home. Start right where you are. Family, friends, and neighbors are the first who should experience our witness to abundant life. You don't need to go down to a street corner, or go knocking on doors. Start in Jerusalem. Start right at home.

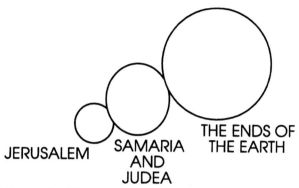

Figure 1: The spread of the gospel in Acts 1:8

Next you can move out to Samaria and Judea. (See figure 1.) The second stage in witnessing is to move beyond the local to a bit of a wider range. And finally, Jesus says, be my witnesses to all the ends of the earth. Some may be called to go abroad. If you hear that call, God bless you as you respond. But if you do not get to all the ends of the earth, do not feel that you are less of a witness. Jesus needs his witnesses in Jerusalem. Jesus needs his witnesses right here at home just as much as he needs missionaries to the ends of the earth.

THINK ABOUT IT

How does the concept of being a witness for Jesus affect your understanding of evangelism?

Are you comfortable talking to your family and closest friends about your faith? Why or why not?

What steps can you take to be a witness for Christ in your own home, in your own family?

TRY IT OUT

Our role as witnesses begins at home. Try to take a little time today and talk about your faith with those who are closest to you. Talk to your husband, your wife, your best friend, your child, or your parent about Jesus. Ask them to tell you a little about their faith as well. Don't argue or convince or try to change. Simply talk and share together. There is no need to witness in Samaria and Judea and the ends of the earth if we are not yet witnesses at home in Jerusalem.

GROUP MEETING FOR WEEK 1

Praying together

Review of this week's material

Exercises, role plays, or case studies

Divide into three small groups of three to five persons. Assign a case study to each group and take five to ten minutes to discuss the case and answer the questions. Have each small group report to the larger group on their discussion and conclusions. (Larger groups can have more than three smaller groups. More than one sub-group will focus on each case.)

Case #1

The pastor of your church has called a meeting of the Evangelism Committee to train them in the task of evangelism. He gives a pep talk and tells them about the importance of doing evangelism. His pep talk goes something like this: "You and I have the most important job in the life of the church. We are called to evangelize. This is important. This is essential. Our denomination is losing members. We are having trouble paying all of our bills and funding all of our missionaries. Let's make our church grow. Let's get new members and new money here so we can be an example to our denomination and show them how it's done. Let's go evangelize."

> What is right in this case?
> What is wrong with this case?
> What would you do differently?

Case #2

A Christian friend invites you to go out and do some evangelizing with him. You have never evangelized door-to-door and are curious to find out how it is done, so you agree to go along. As you approach the first door you are a little unsure but your friend is very confident. The door opens and your friend begins, "Good evening. I am Jim Smith from Our Savior Church. I have a question for you. If you die tonight, are you sure you will go to Heaven?"

> What is right in this case?
> What is wrong with this case?
> What would you do differently?

Case #3

You are curious about evangelism and choose to talk about it with two of your Christian friends. Friend number one tells you that he is an evangelist because over the last twelve months, he has saved 47 souls. He shows you a notebook with dates and names. He tells you that each person in his book prayed a prayer accepting Jesus as Lord and Savior after one or more encounters with him. He does not know where more than eight or ten of them are these days. Friend number two also tells you he is an evangelist. He tells you about the time he sat with his elderly next-door neighbor and held her hand after her husband died. He mentions the time a co-worker was going through a divorce. They ate lunch together once a week for two months and at the end of their meal, he offered a brief, simple prayer for her. He mentions the new family that came into the neighborhood. He invited them to Sunday School and church and even sat with them at worship and led the children to their classes.

> Which of these two is a real evangelist?
> Why or why not?

Telling our story

Leader Input
A Gospel Mandate

Invite someone from your group to read the Great Commission passage as it appears in Matthew 28:16-20.

This is probably the most well-known of the four Great Commission passages. We use it frequently when we want to make the point that Christians are called to do evangelism.

After your group has read this passage from Matthew, ask persons to find a partner and discuss what this scripture has to say about evangelism. Give them five minutes to brainstorm as teams of two. When they have finished talking together, invite them to share what they have learned. List on the board the results of these discussions.

The first thing you will want to note is that the Great Commission passages are **mandates** to do evangelism. Jesus does not offer the Great Commission as a suggestion. He doesn't say, "If you feel like it, you might consider sharing the gospel and making disciples." This is a commandment. These are our marching orders. Jesus is just about to ascend to be with God and these are his final words to his followers. He is about to entrust his church, his mission, and his life's work into their hands. Here is how he wants them to do it.

Some points that should emerge in your discussion of this passage include the following:

- Jesus calls on his followers to "make disciples." Note that he does not say, "Go and make converts." There is a difference between a disciple and a convert. Converts are persons who simply profess to follow Jesus Christ. Disciples undertake a whole new way of live, a way of life that encompasses every aspect of who they are and what they do. Jesus' mandate is to "Go and make disciples!"
- A second point that you will note is that this evangelistic outreach involves teaching. This is not just teaching about Jesus. It is teaching the new disciple to "obey everything that I have commanded you." This is an awesome challenge. We are called to teach disciples to obey Jesus...to follow his commands. Again, this has to do with all of life. His commands include forgiving the sinner, caring about the poor, reaching out to the outcast, and using our possessions in a responsible manner. This is a lot more than simply getting a person to say, "Yes, I believe in Jesus."
- The third point we need to understand from this Great Commission passage is that we are not alone as we do this work. Jesus says, "I am with you always, to the end of the age." The evangelism task is not something we do by ourselves; we are accompanied and empowered by the risen Christ.

There may be other points that persons in your group will glean from this encounter with the scriptures. The important thing is to recognize the gospel mandate to evangelize and the richness of what constitutes the evangelistic encounter.

Assignments
   Visits to prospects, shut-ins
   Telling our story next week
   Testimonies at worship

Closing prayer time

Evaluation

OVERCOMING BARRIERS AND OBSTACLES

DAY ONE: *There Is No One Method*

This week we are going to spend a little time looking at some of the reasons we may not talk about Jesus or witness to our faith. There may be many reasons that make you hesitant to speak out about Jesus Christ. We will explore some of those and you will also have the opportunity to think about some that are not lifted up in these pages. Finally, we hope to offer some constructive suggestions that will aid you as you move beyond those concerns that are barriers and obstacles to your own evangelism.

One concern you may have that makes you hesitate to evangelize is a concern about method. You wonder if you are using the "right method." You wonder if there are certain magic words, special prayers, or Bible verses you must know before you are competent or able to tell someone else about your faith. Too often, a concern about the "right" method gets in the way, and the good news doesn't get out.

Last week we already saw that there are a variety of methods in evangelism. We looked at several models. Andrew, Philip, and Barnabas gave us three models of evangelism. Each one of these is valid and effective. You may find that one style is more suited to you. Or you may find that as situations change and different occasions arise, you may switch from one style of talking about Jesus to another style that better suits the occasion. The good news today is that there are countless ways to tell the good news. You do not need to be limited to one particular, right method.

Even God uses different methods with different people in different situations. Luke tells the story of some unnamed disciples who were walking to Emmaus on the first Easter Sunday (Luke 24:13-32, NRSV):

> Now that same day two of them were going to a village called Emmaus, about seven miles from Jerusalem, and talking with each other about all these things that had happened. While they were talking and discussing, Jesus himself came near and went with them, but their eyes were kept from recognizing him. And he said to them, "What are you discussing with each other while you walk along?" They stood still, looking sad. Then one of them, whose name was Cleopas, answered him, "Are you the only stranger

in Jerusalem who does not know the things that have taken place there in these days?" He asked them, "What things?" They replied, "The things about Jesus of Nazareth, who was a prophet mighty in deed and word before God and all the people, and how our chief priests and leaders handed him over to be condemned to death and crucified him. But we had hoped that he was the one to redeem Israel. Yes, and besides all this, it is now the third day since these things took place. Moreover, some women of our group astounded us. They were at the tomb early this morning, and when they did not find his body there, they came back and told us that they had indeed seen a vision of angels who said that he was alive. Some of those who were with us went to the tomb and found it just as the women had said; but they did not see him." Then he said to them, "Oh, how foolish you are, and how slow of heart to believe all that the prophets have declared! Was it not necessary that the Messiah should suffer these things and then enter into his glory?" Then beginning with Moses and all the prophets, he interpreted to them the things about himself in all the scriptures.

As they came near the village to which they were going, he walked ahead as if he were going on. But they urged him strongly, saying, "Stay with us, because it is almost evening and the day is now nearly over." So he went in to stay with them. When he was at the table with them, he took bread, blessed and broke it, and gave it to them. Then their eyes were opened and they recognized him; and he vanished from their sight. They said to each other, "Were not our hearts burning within us while he was talking to us on the road, while he was opening the scriptures to us?"

The Emmaus experience is one way God, through Jesus Christ, shared good news and opened the eyes of the unbelieving, grieving disciples to faith. Through a quiet discussion, by discussing the scriptures, and finally, through a shared meal, their eyes were opened and they recognized their companion as the risen Messiah.

Tomorrow we will look at another, totally different, method God used to reach the one who was perhaps the hardest one God ever had to reach.

THINK ABOUT IT
Do you worry about using the right method in your efforts to witness about Jesus Christ?

What are some of your specific methodological concerns? Bible knowledge? Theological concepts? The right words? Others?

What are other barriers and obstacles that get in the way of your evangelizing?

TRY IT OUT

Get together with another member of the group this week. Try to visit at home or go out for a snack. (If you can't get together, at least talk on the telephone). Discuss together some of your common concerns, barriers, and obstacles to talking about Jesus. See if you can come up with some ways to overcome them.

DAY TWO: *No One Method-Part Two*

Yesterday we saw one method God used to open the disciples' eyes to Jesus. That method involved discussion, the exposition of scriptures, and a shared meal. Eventually, there was a realization of who was in their midst. The disciples' eyes were opened. They recognized the risen Christ...and they believed. This was a gradual process of coming to faith.

In Acts 9, Luke gives another story of conversion. In this story, an individual comes to faith and has his eyes opened. The process is not slow and gradual, but instead sudden and dramatic. Here is the story of Saul's conversion as found in Acts 9 (NRSV):

> Meanwhile Saul, still breathing threats and murder against the disciples of the Lord, went to the high priest and asked him for letters to the synagogues at Damascus, so that if he found any who belonged to the Way, men or women, he might bring them bound to Jerusalem. Now as he was going along and approaching Damascus, suddenly a light from heaven flashed around him. He fell to the ground and heard a voice saying to him, "Saul, Saul, why do you persecute me?" He asked, "Who are you, Lord?" The reply came, "I am Jesus, whom you are persecuting. But get up and enter the city, and you will be told what you are to do." The men who were traveling with him stood speechless because they heard the voice but saw no one. Saul got up from the ground, and though his eyes were open, he could see nothing so they led him by the hand and brought him to Damascus. For three days he was without sight, and neither ate nor drank.
>
> Now there was a disciple in Damascus named Ananias. The Lord said to him in a vision, "Ananias." He answered, "Here I am, Lord." The Lord said to him, "Get up and go to the street called Straight, and at the house of Judas look for a man of Tarsus named Saul. At this moment he is praying, and he has seen in a vision a man named Ananias come in and lay his hands on him so that he might regain his sight." But Ananias answered, "Lord, I have heard from many about this man, how much evil he has done to your saints in Jerusalem; and here he has authority from the chief priests

to bind all who invoke your name." But the Lord said to him, "Go, for he is an instrument whom I have chosen to bring my name before Gentiles and kings and before the people of Israel; I myself will show him how much he must suffer for the sake of my name." So Ananias went and entered the house. He laid his hands on Saul and said, "Brother Saul, the Lord Jesus, who appeared to you on your way here, has sent me so that you may regain your sight and be filled with the Holy Spirit." And immediately something like scales fell from his eyes, and his sight was restored. Then he got up and was baptized, and after taking some food, he regained his strength.

Yesterday and today we saw two quite distinct conversion stories. In each, God used a method that was distinct from the other. Yet, both methods proved effective. In both cases, the good news was shared, lives were changed, and the power of new life in Jesus Christ was experienced.

When you are concerned about needing to master a specific method before you can evangelize and talk about Jesus, remember these two stories. There is no one method for sharing good news. God can use different people and distinct methods, and the gospel is still proclaimed.

THINK ABOUT IT
What differences strike you about the stories we read yesterday and today?

How do your willingness and readiness to do evangelism change when you realize that there is no one right method?

TRY IT OUT
If you have not yet set a time to get together with another class member, do so today.

DAY THREE: *Evangelism Happens Right Where You Are*

A couple of months ago, I was in the sanctuary of our church on a weekday afternoon. I was taking a break from the office, seeking a chance for a little solitude, quiet, and prayer.

I hadn't been there long when there was a knock at the door leading into the hallway. The door opened and there stood a young man. He had the biggest, brightest smile I had ever seen. I greeted him and asked how I could help him, uncertain if he was there with a concern, or with a business proposition.

He came to where I was standing, and then, just as if a switch had been flipped on, he began his presentation. "Good afternoon, sir. I am Archie Smith, from Pascagoula, Mississippi. It certainly is a lovely day today, isn't it? And what a wonderful church you have here. This is one of the most beautiful churches I have ever seen. Sir, I am here to share something exciting and wonderful with you today. Now if you were to look at me to see what is exciting and wonderful, what would you pick out? You would probably pick out my necktie, right? Isn't this a beautiful tie? It really brightens things up. But what I have to share with you today is really brighter and better then even my necktie. What I have to share with you is my special blend of all-purpose, non-toxic, cleaning solution. Here it is." (He pulls a squeeze bottle from his bag.) "Look at this. It doesn't make you sick?" (He places part of the nozzle in his mouth.) "And it cleans even the toughest stains. Here, let me polish your brass candlestick and show you just what this amazing stuff will do."

Mr. Archie Smith from Pascagoula, Mississippi, obviously had a prepared approach he used to sell his cleaning solution. It was evident to me from his greeting, his too-big smile, and his remarks about his necktie. All I had to do was give a nod, say yes at the right time, or give another encouraging signal, and he was off on the next phase of his presentation.

My experience with Mr. Smith is not unlike the experiences some of us have had with Christians who wish to talk to us about Jesus. Their speech is prepared. All we need to do is nod, say yes, and respond a little, and they are launched into the next phase of their presentation. They are selling Jesus in the same way others sell cleaning solution. In fact, the same presentation might work with either one; just substitute the product, Jesus, for cleaning solution, and everything else stays pretty much the same.

Such canned sales techniques are often another obstacle in our efforts to talk about Jesus. If we have experienced such techniques firsthand, we avoid evangelism because we don't want to be a party to such presentations of that which purports to be the gospel. Or perhaps we think that this is the way it must be done, and we aren't comfortable giving such canned presentations, so we shy away from and avoid talking about Jesus.

The good news today is that making a canned presentation, or handing out a tract, or knocking on doors are not the best, most effective evangelism techniques. Don't worry if you can't remember or memorize a presentation. Don't shy away from talking about Jesus because you can't smile and turn on a rehearsed sales pitch. Don't hesitate to evangelize because you are uncomfortable knocking on the doors of strangers.

The most effective form of evangelism is evangelism that flows from the heart and life of the believer. It is evangelism that is fleshed out in the believer's life. It is not something we try to sell to strangers, but something we live out in the midst of relationships, friendships, and family. Those who benefit most from our sharing of good news are not those we meet for a few brief moments with a sales pitch on their doorstep. Those who experience our evangelism as good news are those whose lives intersect ours, those who know we care about them, those who see our words enfleshed in the grace of Christ as we live out our day to day lives in their midst.

Your presentation may be stuttering. It may be unrehearsed. But it can be very effective when it is shared and enacted out of love in the midst of relationships you have cultivated and friendships you treasure. Rebecca Pippert writes, "By far the most effective, the most costly, and even perhaps the most biblical kind of evangelism is found in the person or groups who look at the people around them, those with whom their own life naturally intersects and then begin to cultivate friendships and to love them."[5]

Evangelism isn't a smiling transaction with a stranger, akin to selling cleaning solution. It involves cultivating trust, friendship, and relationship, and then, out of love, acting out the good news that is Christ.

THINK ABOUT IT

Studies have shown that most people who join churches attend and join because they have been invited by a friend. The invitation of a friend ranks ahead of dynamic preaching, visits from the pastor, direct mail, advertising, or other outreach methods. Why do you think that this is?

How do you respond to the idea that evangelism is more a matter of reaching out to those whose lives intersect ours as opposed to making rehearsed presentations to strangers?

TRY IT OUT

Try to think of three persons to whom you could reach out. Look at your network of friends, co-workers, neighbors, and family members. A very non-threatening way to reach

---

[5]Rebecca Pippert, Out of the Salt Shaker (Downer's Grove, Ill.: Intervarsity, 1979), 174.

out to them is to extend an invitation to visit at your church. Invite them to join you this
Sunday. List them here:

1
2
3

DAY FOUR: *No Need to Fear*

In addition to being a parish pastor, I serve as an Army Chaplain with the Virginia Army
National Guard. Once or twice a year, part of my Army training involves repelling down a
repelling tower. Repelling is the process of attaching one's body to a rope, stepping off
the top of a platform, and then lowering oneself to the ground.

Needless to say, every time I go repelling, I am somewhat afraid. No matter how many
times I have done it, no matter that I have never had an accident, every time I am ready to
step over the edge of that tower, my heart beats rapidly, I breathe deeply, and my stomach
gets tied up in knots. There is a certain level of fear that is present each time I step off the
tower.

My fear is tempered somewhat by the knowledge that nothing bad can really happen to
me. The rope that is attached to my body is also firmly secured at the top of the tower.
Even if I were somehow to lose my grip on the rope and begin to fall, my fall would be
broken because the rope is anchored to the top of the tower. It is not going anywhere.
That bit of knowledge helps put my fear in perspective.

I think that one obstacle we encounter in our attempts to talk about Jesus is fear. An
opportunity to discuss our faith presents itself, and our heart rate goes up, and our
stomach gets into knots. We are afraid. We are afraid that we will somehow say the
wrong thing. We are afraid the person we are talking to will not be interested, or will
throw down a challenging question. We are afraid of the outcome of the encounter.

Fear is a natural reaction, whether you are stepping off a tower, or sharing the gospel of
Jesus. Over time, as you get more comfortable with either activity, the fear will likely
diminish.

However, just as the rope can provide security to me as I go off the repelling tower, there
is also a source of security for the one who shares the gospel. That source of security is
what John Wesley called God's "Prevenient Grace."

Prevenient Grace is the grace of God that goes before us. It assures us that in any
encounter of sharing the good news, God has already been there. God has been involved

preparing the way. You are not alone as you minister the gospel to another. God has already been active in that person's life in quiet, perhaps unseen, unnoticed ways. But Prevenient Grace is there. You have no need to tremble in fear.

Prevenient grace is God's ever-present grace. It is the grace of God manifested through our consciences. The noted Methodist scholar Albert Outler says, "Human life is meaningfully related to God even in sin and estrangement. The sinner has some dim, imperfect knowledge of God in his fleeting moments of transcendental or mystical awareness; his moral conscience is deadened but not destroyed."[6] Prevenient grace is the grace that compels good works, even from unsaved persons. John Wesley would argue that good works are not possible on one's own. It is only through the action of prevenient grace that one who is not a follower of Jesus Christ can be capable of good works.

This prevenient grace is always present. Outler continues, "It is not just that God loves us no matter what (although he does) but that his grace surrounds and anticipates us in every crisis, from birth to death, creating and holding open possibilities of growth and healing and self-fulfillment."[7]

This is reassuring to you and me as we go about the work of sharing good news. We are not alone. We can talk about Jesus in the full knowledge that prevenient grace goes with us, indeed it goes ahead of us. Our hearers are already being affected by God's prevenient grace.

THINK ABOUT IT
Do you experience fear when you talk to others about your faith?

How does that fear manifest itself?

How does the knowledge of prevenient grace affect your ability or desire to share good news?

---

[6]Albert C. Outler, Evangelism in the Wesleyan Spirit (Nashville: Tidings, 1971), 45.
[7]Ibid.

TRY IT OUT
Have you visited with another class member yet?
Have you invited a friend to worship yet?
Use today to complete the tasks of days one-three.

DAY FIVE: *Encountering Other Religions*

You and I live in what is called a pluralistic society. Ours is an open society. Chances are that in our communities, in our schools, and at our workplaces, we will encounter persons of other religious beliefs. Some of our best friends or our children's playmates may be Muslim, Hindu, Buddhist, or Jewish. How do we share our good news with those whose religions are distinctly different from our own?

One school of thought argues that there is no need to share our faith with those of other religions. This view suggests that all religions are equally valid. All religions are equally true. No matter whether one is a Christian, or a Muslim, or a Hindu, all are headed on the same path to the same place. We are all climbing the same mountain and, through different paths, will end up at the same destination. If this is your position, there is no need to witness. There is no need to talk about Jesus with persons of other faiths. Indeed, their faith is simply another option to Christianity and they are both equally true.

A second school of thought is directly the opposite. According to this way of thinking, all other religions are totally wrong. Persons following other religions are lost. Thus, they need to be confronted aggressively and converted.

Both of these ways of thinking affect how we do evangelism and talk about Jesus. The first school of thought says evangelism is unnecessary. Thus, we never discuss our faith with those of other religions. The other school of thought says those of other faiths are wrong and need to be challenged and changed. Embracing this approach may hinder our evangelism efforts because we are not comfortable confronting other's beliefs and calling them into question.

A third approach takes something of a middle ground. This third approach sees Jesus Christ as God's unique, supreme, decisive Savior of the world. Because of Jesus Christ, God's Kingdom has been inaugurated and will someday be fulfilled. Thus, Jesus Christ is indeed different from other religious figures down through the centuries. He is supreme. Not all religions are equal. Jesus is the one who brings God's ultimate Kingdom.

A healthy attitude toward other religions sees those religions as seeking and wanting to move toward the ultimate kingdom that God has promised in Jesus Christ. This does not mean that Christians must view other religions as enemies of the gospel. Instead, they are in quest of the future that we are promised in Jesus Christ. We can believe that God is working in and through those other faiths to prepare them to encounter the ultimate kingdom God announces in Jesus Christ. Other religions are not necessarily enemies of Jesus Christ. But they are, however, in need of the fulfillment that Jesus Christ alone offers. Some have compared other religions to John the Baptist, preparing the way for the coming of Christ.

Carl Braaten, a Lutheran scholar, compares the other religions to a road sign along the highway.[8] The signs are set up on the side of the highway, but in the darkness of the night, they do not make any sense unless they are illuminated by a car's headlight. Likewise, the religions of the world are all around us. But they are not complete, they are not fully illuminated, they do not fully make sense in an ultimate way until they have been illuminated by the light of Jesus Christ. The good news of God's kingdom in Jesus Christ needs to be announced to all the world, including those of other religions who are still looking and striving, but do not know what God has done in Jesus.

This is not a call for us to confront or challenge the beliefs of others. Indeed, we can appreciate them and try to see points of commonality with Christianity where God is working in and through their religion. (Remember prevenient grace? Perhaps we can see that God's prevenient grace is operating in and through other religions). At the same time, we need not shy away from dialoging with those of other faiths and telling them the good news of Jesus. He is the fulfillment of what they are seeking. He is God's ultimate message to God's world.

THINK ABOUT IT

How do you think of other religions? Are all equal? Is there something different about Jesus?

Have you ever discussed your faith with a person of a different religion? Why or why not?

How has today's discussion helped you in your understanding of Christianity and other religions of the world?

---

[8]Carl E. Braaten, No Other Gospel! (Minneapolis: Augsburg Fortress, 1992), 71.

TRY IT OUT

If you have a friend or acquaintance of another religion, invite him or her to talk with you today. Ask them about their religion. Tell them a little about why you are a Christian. If you have no opportunity to do this, take another sheet of paper and write up an imaginary discussion with a person of another faith. How might you invite him or her to talk about the Christian faith?

DAY SIX: *Wesley's "Scripture Way of Salvation"*

It is helpful to gain insight into evangelism by looking at what John Wesley called "The Scripture Way of Salvation." Wesley's model gives an understanding of both the nature and process of salvation. Sometimes United Methodists may feel that they must look outside their tradition to find an understanding of the process of salvation. Many times we are unaware that the Wesleyan tradition offers what is perhaps the classic understanding of the process of salvation. John Wesley's "Scripture Way of Salvation" is central to a working understanding of evangelism.

Prevenient Grace. The first step in John Wesley's scripture way of salvation depends on the action of "prevenient grace." (Recall our discussion of prevenient grace on Day Four.) Prevenient grace, or preventing grace, to use the traditional term, is that grace which goes before. It is God's grace that is available to all, whether they realize it or not. It is the grace of God manifested through our consciences, the grace that compels good works, even from unsaved persons.

Prevenient grace is the "porch" of religion. It stands out front of one's spiritual life, preparing one for a fuller encounter with God, a more specific experience of God's grace. Prevenient grace nudges us, unsettles us, and makes us search for something more, something deeper in life. Prevenient grace helps us to realize our need for Christ's salvation.

Justifying Grace. After one understands the need for God and salvation in one's life, one moves on to the second of Wesley's three concepts of grace: justifying grace. If prevenient grace is the "porch" of a person's spiritual life, justifying grace serves as the "door." It is the entrance through which one goes to experience the salvation offered in Jesus Christ.

43

While the first stage may lead to a sense of discomfort or even fear because of a sense of guilt before God, justifying grace leads one to a sense of joy, a sense of forgiveness, and a sense of peace . Wesley writes, "The immediate effects of justification are, the peace of God, a 'peace that passeth all understanding,' and a 'rejoicing in the hope of the glory of God' with 'joy unspeakable and full of glory.'"[9]

Justifying grace is experienced through faith in Christ. When one places his or her faith in Christ, and experiences justification, one basically experiences pardon and forgiveness. Specifically, Wesley says, "Justification is another word for pardon. It is the forgiveness of all our sins; and what is necessarily implied therein, our acceptance with God."[10]

Sanctifying Grace. Justification is the experience of being made right with God. One has crossed over the porch of prevenient grace and passed through the doorway of justifying grace. The new believer has experienced forgiveness and, many times, assurance that he or she has been saved, forgiven, and set right with God. However, while that change in status does occur and is very real, it is still possible to continue in sin. It is possible to stray back into old habits and practices. Thus, there is a need for the third kind of grace: sanctifying grace. Sanctifying grace becomes the "living room" of one's faith, the place where that faith is lived out on a day-to-day basis.

Sanctifying grace is the grace experienced throughout the whole of one's life as a follower of Jesus Christ. Sanctifying grace is experienced through the process that is called sanctification. At the moment one is justified (forgiven, set in a right relationship with God), sanctification begins. This sanctification is the life-long process of growing, being transformed, and being made more and more into the image of Jesus Christ.

While justifying grace offers the experience and reality of forgiveness, the need for sanctification is still present. Wesley says that one experiences justification and then "it is seldom long before they are undeceived, finding sin was only suspended, not destroyed. Temptations return, and sin revives; showing it was stunned before, not dead."[11] Thus, there is the need for the process of sanctification. Through the presence of sanctifying grace, the power of the Holy Spirit, and a disciplined life, the process of sanctification begins and continues. Wesley writes, "It is thus that we wait for entire sanctification; for a full salvation from all our sins, from pride, self-will, anger, unbelief; or as the Apostle expresses it, 'go on unto perfection.'"[12] One does not achieve perfection on one's own, but perfection is made possible through the sanctifying grace offered by God.

---

[9]Albert C. Outler ed., John Wesley, (New York: Oxford University Press, 1964), 274.
[10]Ibid., 273.
[11]Ibid., 274.
[12]Ibid., 275.

THINK ABOUT IT

Can you think of times you have witnessed or experienced the three kinds of grace mentioned by John Wesley?

How does John Wesley's understanding of salvation deepen your understanding of evangelism?

TRY IT OUT

Over the next couple of weeks we will be talking a little bit about our own individual faith stories. Spend some time today thinking about your faith story. What does it mean to you to have a relationship with Jesus? What are some landmark moments in that relationship?

DAY SEVEN: *Christ at the Center*

The starting point for all of our evangelism is Jesus Christ. It is possible that a lack of understanding about Jesus and his significance may be a barrier to effective evangelism. If we do not understand who he is, what he has done, and what he promises to do, we cannot be effective evangelists. Why tell others about Jesus, why offer them good news, if we do not understand the centrality and finality of Christ? Jesus Christ is **the decisive** factor in God's outreach to humankind.

Orthodox Christianity holds that in Jesus Christ, God has taken the first step toward relationship and salvation. Jesus Christ is how we come to know about and understand God. Without Jesus Christ, there is no normative way to know who or what God is.

The theologian Wolfhart Pannenburg states, "If God is revealed through Jesus Christ, then who or what God is becomes defined only by the Christ-event...the essence of God is not accessible at all without Jesus Christ."[13]

---

[13]Wolfhart Pannenburg, Jesus-God and Man, trans. Lewis L. Wilkins and Duane A. Priebe (Philadelphia: Westminster Press, 1968), 130, quoted in Braaten, 75.

In Jesus Christ, God has acted first to reach out to humanity. All we do is respond. In many religious faiths, human effort is the starting point. Humans make the effort to get in touch with God. In Christianity, God has first reached out to humans.

Theologian Carl Braaten writes,

> Somehow Christ is the place where the contradiction between God and humanity gets resolved-actually and necessarily. In this one person, Jesus Christ-through his life, ministry, death, and resurrection-salvation is effected for the world through the outpouring of the love of God, who overcomes his wrath and enables the "happy exchange" to take place. Christ does not merely tell the world of God's love; he makes it happen by reconciling God and the world to each other. Something actually has to happen as the necessary condition and efficient cause of salvation, and the locus of this happening is Christ alone.[14]

All of this is to say that in Jesus Christ, God does something that is unique, decisive, and final. God has reached out to the world with salvation, forgiveness, and abundant life. When one looks at Jesus Christ, a man hanging on a cross, paying the price in order to bring in the Kingdom, one cannot help but realize that something divine and unique is going on here.

Thus, all evangelism begins with Jesus Christ. He is the center. He is what it is all about. He is the good news that we share. The work of God in Christ is so powerful, so decisive, and so important that he overcomes the barriers and calls us to share the good news.

THINK ABOUT IT

What makes Jesus Christ God's final, unique, decisive outreach to humanity?
Why is this kind of strong understanding of Jesus so essential to evangelism?

Where are you in overcoming the barriers you face in talking about Jesus? Which ones still loom large?

---

[14] Reprinted by permission from No Other Gospel by Carl Braaten, copyright 1992, Augsburg Fortress, 77.

TRY IT OUT
Write these words, **"JESUS CHRIST...THE CENTER OF IT ALL,"** on a 3x5 card.
Keep this card in your pocket or purse. Look at it as often as you can throughout the day.

GROUP MEETING FOR WEEK 2

Praying together

Review of this week's material

Exercises, role plays, or case studies
Divide into three small groups. Take five minutes or so to read your assigned case and
develop a brief skit that dramatizes your case. Present your skit to the entire group.

Case #1
Develop a skit that dramatizes an evangelistic encounter that is poor, offensive, or
insensitive.

Case #2
Develop a skit in which you invite a friend, relative, or neighbor to visit your church.

Case #3
Develop a skit in which you encounter a person of another faith.

Telling our story

Leader Input
The Building Blocks of the Gospel

An important way to share the good news is actually to know and relate the essential
elements of the gospel. This is not to say that you have a canned "sales pitch" that uses
certain rehearsed phrases and Bible verses as you present the gospel to unsuspecting
listeners. What I am suggesting, however, is that you be familiar with the key "building
blocks" of the gospel message. You understand these building blocks and are familiar
with them to the extent that when an opportunity to discuss the good news presents itself,
you will be able to bring the gospel message to bear on that situation.

For example, suppose that you are out to lunch with a co-worker. She has been absent for several days and seems kind of distracted. Using your active listening skills, you express your concern and invite her to share what is on her mind. She begins to open up to you and confides to you that she had become pregnant and has just had an abortion. She is dealing with feelings of guilt. She wonders if she has made a terrible mistake. She wonders if she can ever forgive herself for what she has done and if she is a terrible person. In spite of how you may view abortion, you offer your unconditional love and do not judge. Here is an opportunity to share a little good news. You know that one of the building blocks of the gospel is a God who forgives, a God who offers second chances, a God of unconditional love. This was demonstrated on the cross and at the resurrection. You share with your friend these truths about God's love, you act them out in your own acceptance and love, and you offer to pray with her. You promise to be there to listen and simply sit with her anytime.

You have just evangelized. You have just shared good news. Your knowledge of the essential building blocks of the gospel message allowed you to share a bit of God's story at the point where it could intersect with her story and make a difference in her life.

Next week you we will examine the building blocks of the gospel message in some depth. We will also explore ways those building blocks can be brought to bear on the situations of those with whom we share our faith.
Without looking ahead to next week's lessons, do a little brainstorming. Write here what you would perceive to be the essential building blocks of the gospel message. If you were to distill the Biblical Story to its bare essentials, what would they be?

-
-
-
-
-
-
-

Assignments
Visits to prospects, shut-ins
Telling our story next week
Testimonies at worship

Closing prayer time

Evaluation

THE BUILDING BLOCKS OF THE GOSPEL MESSAGE

DAY ONE: *A Good God Created a Good Creation*

This week we will attempt to boil the Christian faith down to its basic essentials. We will call these the "Building Blocks of the Gospel Message." The goal of this week is for you to come to understand and grasp these seven essential points.

If you are going to share the good news, it is imperative that you understand what the good news is. Granted, theologians have studied the Christian faith for centuries. Entire libraries have been filled with writings about the meaning of Christianity. I do not expect that as a result of this week you will be a theological scholar who is able to discuss the deepest nuances of the faith. The idea of this week is simply to get a clearer understanding of what it is we believe and share. By distilling the message into seven essential "building blocks" you will be better able to talk about what it is you believe and share the good news with one who is seeking.

These seven basic "building blocks" are not something for you to memorize and recite as a scripted presentation when you share the gospel. They are not a list of seven steps to salvation. These are simply the basic points of the gospel for you to use when you are able as you interact with those around you. I do not suggest that you sit down with a friend and pull out a card and proceed to lead him or her through these seven points. Instead, I suggest that as you listen and converse, you look for little opportunities to tell the good news by making reference to one or two of these points.

For example, suppose that you are having dinner with a group of friends who may or may not be Christians. The talk turns to how terrible the world is. Everyone agrees that drugs, crime, and violence have made this a pretty hopeless place to live. This is your opening to interject a little good news into the conversation. You think back to the seven "building blocks" you learned in this study and recall that one of them had to do with the hope of God's Kingdom. You add your input to the conversation when you comment, "Yes, the world sure does look like a pretty bad place. Fortunately, I have a brighter outlook on it all. God promised that one day Christ will return to judge the evil and restore the world to perfection. That is what helps me from being totally depressed by it all."

The conversation may pick up on this comment and you will have the opportunity to develop this thought further, or the conversation may continue in another direction. In either case, you have shared a bit of good news and maybe provoked some thought about God's promises. The "building blocks" were the essential tool that enabled you to interject some good news into the conversation.

The wonderful thing about learning and understanding the seven building blocks is that you don't need to memorize lots of Bible verses or theological teachings. All you need to do is have a grasp of the building block itself. We will look at scriptures that back it up. You may want to be familiar with some of these. The verses we are using this week are from the New International Version of the Bible. But the only thing you really need to know and be able to discuss is the building block itself and what it is about. If you grasp the building block, you have a grasp of one of the essential truths of Christianity that is affirmed throughout the Bible.

Today we will look at the first building block: **A Good God Created a Good Creation.** The scriptures affirm in many places that God is the force behind creation. Some of those scriptures are listed here.

Genesis 1:31: God saw all that he had made, and it was very good. And there was evening, and there was morning-the sixth day.

Isaiah 45:18: For this is what the LORD says-
he who created the heavens,
  he is God;
he who fashioned and made the earth,
  he founded it;
he did not create it to be empty,
  but formed it to be inhabited-
he says:
"I am the LORD,
  and there is no other.

Colossians 1:16: For by him all things were created: things in heaven and on earth, visible and invisible, whether thrones or powers or rulers or authorities; all things were created by him and for him.

The "building block" of creation is essential because it establishes that God is behind all that has been created and when it was created, it was good. We don't profess to be scientists, knowing just how it was created. But we hold to the belief that God did the creating and that the creation was perfect. Creation and all that was in it was just what God desired.

The "building block" of creation tells us that humankind was created in God's own image. Thus we are precious and special, like God himself. It is God who sustains the creation and God who continues to create through the miracles of creation we experience around us every day. God loves God's creation and will not abandon it.

THINK ABOUT IT

Today's "Building Block" is: **A Good God Created a Good Creation**. Write in your own words what that means to you.

Envision some of the interactions and conversations you have in a typical week. What are some occasions when you might be able to share a little good news by mentioning your belief that a good God created a good creation?

- Talking with someone about the birth of his or her child
- Looking at a beautiful sunset with a friend
-
-
-
-

TRY IT OUT

Take an index card and on the top write "BUILDING BLOCKS OF THE GOSPEL."

Write today's building block beside the number 1. Look at your card throughout the day and remind yourself of this key building block.

Keep alert today for opportunities you might have to talk about God's goodness and God's good creation. Offer this bit of good news into conversations if appropriate opportunities present themselves.

DAY TWO: *Humans Sin; Creation Is Broken*

While God created a perfect creation, it did not stay that way. The beautiful picture was broken by sin. Humans were created with the ability to choose God or to reject God and his love. Men and women use this free will to seek their own destiny apart from God. Each day we still choose to try to make our own way and live apart from God's sustaining love. When we break this relationship between God and ourselves, we are in sin. God, being holy and just, judges this sin. Thus, the broken human creature lives in alienation under the judgment of God.

This sin and brokenness is not just a condition of humans; it extends into all of creation. The whole creation is influenced by and subject to this state of sin. God's perfect creation has become a place of decay, violence, chaos, suffering, and evil. There is violence in the animal kingdom. Nature is being destroyed by pollutants. Nations go to war with one another and in the process destroy the perfect kingdom that was created by God. People starve and go homeless and suffer from terrible diseases.

This is not God's will. As demonstrated in the first building block, God's will is a perfect creation which is good. But God took a risk in giving humans free will and dominion over the earth. Humans abused the free will and now the whole of creation is groaning and suffering. Certainly God must shed tears to see that perfect creation and those beloved creatures doing this to God's precious masterpiece. The issue is not one of a God who can't be good because bad things happen in the world. The issue is that a good God made it good and wants it to be good. Sin entered the picture and is destroying God's creation. The good God is in anguish with and for his creation.

Some scriptures concerning human sin and broken creation with which you may wish to be familiar include:

Mark 7:20: He went on: "What comes out of a man is what makes him 'unclean.' For from within, out of men's hearts, come evil thoughts, sexual immorality, theft, murder, adultery, greed, malice, deceit, lewdness, envy, slander, arrogance and folly. All these evils come from inside and make a man 'unclean.' "

1 John 1:8: If we claim to be without sin, we deceive ourselves and the truth is not in us.

Romans 5:12: Therefore, just as sin entered the world through one man, and death through sin, and in this way death came to all men, because all sinned...

Ephesians 6:10-12: Finally, be strong in the Lord and in his mighty power. Put on the full armor of God so that you can take your stand against the devil's schemes. For our struggle is not against flesh and blood, but against the rulers, against the authorities, against the powers of this dark world and against the spiritual forces of evil in the heavenly realms.

Romans 8:18: I consider that our present sufferings are not worth comparing with the glory that will be revealed in us. The creation waits in eager expectation for the sons of God to be revealed. For the creation was subjected to frustration, not by its own choice, but by the will of the one who subjected it, in hope that the creation itself will be liberated from its bondage to decay and brought into the glorious freedom of the children of God.

THINK ABOUT IT

Today's "Building Block" is: **Humans Sin; Creation Is Broken**. Write in your own words what that means to you.

Envision some of the interactions and conversations you have in a typical week. What are some occasions when you might be able to share a little good news by mentioning your belief that humans sin and creation is broken?

- A person expresses bewilderment at the violence in our world.
- A person questions why there is war, poverty, and hunger.
- You talk to one who is facing a daunting illness...a sign of broken creation.
-
-
-

TRY IT OUT

Take out your index card and write the number 2 and today's building block. Look at your card throughout the day and remind yourself of this key building block.

Keep alert today for opportunities you might have to talk about the fact that humans sin and creation is broken. Offer this as good news by combining it with building block number one: i.e. while sin and brokenness is the reality, it really isn't the way God wants it to be.

DAY THREE: *Jesus of Nazareth*

The reality of sin and brokenness in the world led God to take decisive action. God decided to enter into the world as a man and live among the people a life that embodied God's desire for humanity. Jesus lived the kind of life God wants all of his creatures to live. Jesus is the perfect human that God desired at the start of creation. Jesus of Nazareth is the culmination of many initiatives by God to try to bring this broken world back into line. This Jewish carpenter lived a simple life in Israel teaching, healing, feeding, and, in general, loving and accepting all he met. Jesus exhibited a desire to lift up the outcast and downtrodden. While he loved lepers, beggars, and prostitutes, he had harsh words for the religious leaders and authorities. These leaders only mouthed pious platitudes but did very little to make God's kingdom of love and justice a reality in the world.

When we look at Jesus, we really see what God is like...and we can affirm that God is indeed good. The scriptures are full of references to Jesus of Nazareth, the man who embodied God:

Mark 1:14-15: After John was put in prison, Jesus went into Galilee, proclaiming the good news of God. "The time has come," he said. "The kingdom of God is near. Repent and believe the good news!"

Luke 4:16-21: He went to Nazareth, where he had been brought up, and on the Sabbath day he went into the synagogue, as was his custom. And he stood up to read. The scroll of the prophet Isaiah was handed to him. Unrolling it, he found the place where it is written:

"The Spirit of the Lord is on me,
  because he has anointed me
  to preach good news to the poor.
He has sent me to proclaim freedom for the prisoners
  and recovery of sight for the blind,
to release the oppressed,
to proclaim the year of the Lord's favor."

Then he rolled up the scroll, gave it back to the attendant and sat down. The eyes of everyone in the synagogue were fastened on him, and he began by saying to them, "Today this scripture is fulfilled in your hearing."

John 3:16-17: "For God so loved the world that he gave his one and only Son, that whoever believes in him shall not perish but have eternal life. For God did not send his Son into the world to condemn the world, but to save the world through him.

John 1:14: The Word became flesh and made his dwelling among us. We have seen his glory, the glory of the One and Only, who came from the Father, full of grace and truth.

THINK ABOUT IT
Today's "Building Block" is: **Jesus of Nazareth**. Write in your own words what Jesus of Nazareth means to you.

Envision some of the interactions and conversations you have in a typical week. What are some occasions when you might be able to share a little good news by mentioning your belief in Jesus of Nazareth?
- A discussion about the troubled world might lead you to observe that God does not abandon his creation. He came to this troubled world as the man Jesus.

- A discussion about the plight of the hungry could lead you to discuss God's concern for hunger as demonstrated in Jesus.
-
-

TRY IT OUT

Take out your index card and write the number 3 and today's building block. Look at your card throughout the day and remind yourself of this key building block.

Keep alert today for opportunities you might have to talk about Jesus of Nazareth. Mention him as a bit of good news when appropriate opportunities present themselves.

DAY FOUR: *Jesus Dies on a Cross*

The culmination of Jesus' work took place on a cross. God incarnate, the sinless one, the one who was all that God desired humans to be, was nailed to a cross. Sinful humanity couldn't stand to have this perfect one in their midst, and he was killed by their sin.

The cross says that God shares our suffering. Jesus has experienced the worst that life has to offer. Thus, there can be a solidarity between God and humankind. God has been there, too. Jesus even experienced the pain of being completely abandoned, an experience that many people have in modern times as well.

Jesus on the cross tells us how serious God is about sin. God didn't just look at sin and turn the other way. In the man Jesus, God waded into the filthiness of sin...and ended up being put to death by it. God is that serious about sin, God is that upset by sin, that he is willing to be put to death in his war to overcome it.

In the cross, God makes it possible for humans to experience forgiveness. Jesus "pays the price" that is demanded by a perfect God who abhors sin. That price is death. And the penalty applies to all. Jesus pays the price on behalf of all. Thus, by uniting ourselves with Christ, we need not fear the consequences of sin. Jesus' punishment is borne on our behalf.

Look at some of the scriptures which shed some light on what happened on that cross:

Romans 5:6-8: You see, at just the right time, when we were still powerless, Christ died for the ungodly. Very rarely will anyone die for a righteous man, though for a good man someone might possibly dare to die. But God demonstrates his own love for us in this: While we were still sinners, Christ died for us.

55

2 Corinthians 8:9: For you know the grace of our Lord Jesus Christ, that though he was rich, yet for your sakes he became poor, so that you through his poverty might become rich.

Philippians 2:5-11: Your attitude should be the same as that of Christ Jesus:
Who, being in very nature God,
did not consider equality with God something to be grasped,
but made himself nothing,
taking the very nature of a servant,
being made in human likeness.
And being found in appearance as a man,
he humbled himself
and became obedient to death-
even death on a cross!
Therefore God exalted him to the highest place
and gave him the name that is above every name,
 that at the name of Jesus every knee should bow,
 in heaven and on earth and under the earth,
and every tongue confess that Jesus Christ is Lord,
to the glory of God the Father.

Colossians 1:19-20: For God was pleased to have all his fullness dwell in him, and through him to reconcile to himself all things, whether things on earth or things in heaven, by making peace through his blood, shed on the cross.

THINK ABOUT IT
Today's "Building Block" is: **Jesus Dies on a Cross**. Write in your own words what that means to you.

Envision some of the interactions and conversations you have in a typical week. What are some occasions when you might be able to share a little good news by mentioning your belief that Jesus died on a cross?

- You encounter a person burdened with the guilt of some sinful act. He believes that he could never be forgiven, that nobody, especially not God, could ever love him.
- A person feels totally abandoned as she faces a challenging time in her life. You mention that God can identify with her pain for our God also knows what it is like to be abandoned.
-
-
-
-

TRY IT OUT

Take out your index card and write the number 4 and today's building block. Look at your card throughout the day and remind yourself of this key building block.

Keep alert today for opportunities you might have to talk about Jesus' death on the cross and its ramifications for our lives today. Offer this bit of good news into conversations if appropriate opportunities present themselves.

DAY FIVE: *Jesus Was Raised on the Third Day*

The ultimate culmination of the good news is Jesus' resurrection on the third day. The meaning of the resurrection is awesome. When you stop to ponder it, it is truly overwhelming. Easter is a message of triumph to be celebrated.

First, the resurrection message is our rock in the face of death. Jesus' resurrection tells us that our awesome God is more powerful than even that dark event that we fear most: death. Death is not abandonment. Death is not something to be dreaded. You and I can face our deaths and the deaths of loved ones because we see that in Jesus, God has the power to overcome death. God confronted death face to face, and God won. The resurrection message is good news for a world that is full of death and decay.

The second aspect of the resurrection that is powerfully good news for you and me today is that it tells us of God's triumph over sin. It was sin that nailed that perfect Jesus to the cross. Sin couldn't stand to be confronted by God's holiness, and sought to silence it by putting it to death. For a while, it seemed as if death had won. That was the darkest moment in history. And then on the third day, the stone rolled away and Jesus rose, triumphant over sin. Suddenly Satan, the personification of sin, was trembling with fear. Something more powerful than sin was here. Sin can't keep Jesus down. He triumphs over all that is sinful, evil, broken, and unclean. And as we are united with him, we can claim his power to confront sin. He is the hope for a world that is in the grip of sin. God does still reign. What a message of hope!

As we embrace Jesus as the Lord of our lives, we experience life in the face of death; we have power in the face of sin.

The scriptural images of hope and victory that come because of the resurrection are many. Some of them include:

Romans 6:23: For the wages of sin is death, but the gift of God is eternal life in Christ Jesus our Lord.

Romans 8:31-39: What, then, shall we say in response to this? If God is for us, who can be against us? He who did not spare his own Son, but gave him up for us all-how will he not also, along with him, graciously give us all things? Who will bring any charge against those whom God has chosen? It is God who justifies. Who is he that condemns? Christ Jesus, who died-more than that, who was raised to life-is at the right hand of God and is also interceding for us. Who shall separate us from the love of Christ? Shall trouble or hardship or persecution or famine or nakedness or danger or sword? As it is written:

"For your sake we face death all day long;
we are considered as sheep to be slaughtered."

No, in all these things we are more than conquerors through him who loved us. For I am convinced that neither death nor life, neither angels nor demons, neither the present nor the future, nor any powers, neither height nor depth, nor anything else in all creation, will be able to separate us from the love of God that is in Christ Jesus our Lord.

1 Corinthians 15:3-5: For what I received I passed on to you as of first importance: that Christ died for our sins according to the Scriptures, that he was buried, that he was raised on the third day according to the Scriptures, and that he appeared to Peter, and then to the Twelve.

1 Corinthians 15:51-57: Listen, I tell you a mystery: We will not all sleep, but we will all be changed-in a flash, in the twinkling of an eye, at the last trumpet. For the trumpet will sound, the dead will be raised imperishable, and we will be changed. For the perishable must clothe itself with the imperishable, and the mortal with immortality. When the perishable has been clothed with the imperishable, and the mortal with immortality, then the saying that is written will come true: "Death has been swallowed up in victory." "Where, O death, is your victory? Where, O death, is your sting?" The sting of death is sin, and the power of sin is the law. But thanks be to God! He gives us the victory through our Lord Jesus Christ.

Colossians 1:21-23: Once you were alienated from God and were enemies in your minds because of your evil behavior. But now he has reconciled you by Christ's physical body through death to present you holy in his sight, without blemish and free from accusation-if you continue in your faith, established and firm, not moved from the hope held out in the gospel. This is the gospel that you heard and that has been proclaimed to every creature under heaven, and of which I, Paul, have become a servant.

THINK ABOUT IT

Today's "Building Block" is: **Jesus Was Raised on the Third Day**. Write in your own words what that means to you.

Envision some of the interactions and conversations you have in a typical week. What are some occasions when you might be able to share a little good news by mentioning your belief that Jesus was raised on the third day?

- A person who is dealing with the death of a loved one can draw hope from the resurrection promise of Jesus.
- A discussion of the latest crime report on the 11:00 news can lead to talk about the God who overcomes such terrible sin and crime by triumphing over it on the cross of Christ.
-
-
-
-

TRY IT OUT

Take out your index card and write the number 5 and today's building block. Look at your card throughout the day and remind yourself of this key building block.

Keep alert today for opportunities you might have to talk about the fact that Jesus was raised on the third day. Offer this bit of good news into conversations if appropriate opportunities present themselves.

DAY SIX: *God's Kingdom Is Coming*

The sixth Building Block of the gospel that is essential for us to be familiar with is the powerful truth that God's Kingdom Is Coming. In fact, God's Kingdom is already underway. When Jesus was here on Earth, he began the process of God's Kingdom becoming a reality. His miracles were not just demonstrations of power and love. They were the beginnings of the establishment of God's reign. Jesus inaugurated and pointed toward a day when God will be completely in charge, when evil will be vanquished, and peace and justice will be a reality for all. It will be a time of healing, wholeness, and abundant life.

59

When Jesus ascended, he left those of us who are his followers living in an "in-between" time. We live in the midst of the Kingdom that was begun by Jesus, but we know that it is a far cry from being fulfilled. During this in-between time we have the presence of the Holy Spirit to sustain us, and empower us, and assure us of God's nearness. During this in-between time we have the Church, which is a sign of God's work, presence, and eventual fulfillment. The Church is charged with making the Kingdom more real in the present, and announcing its ultimate fulfillment.

We who are Christians live in the knowledge that this is not all there is. We are always looking forward in hope and confidence. We trust that one day, a day that is only known to God, Jesus Christ will return. That day will be a day of judgment, when all of the evil, corruption, and injustice will be put away once and for all. It will be a day of resurrection and fulfillment and eternal life for those whose trust is in Christ. It will be a joyous day, a day of celebration.

Because of this hope, we can live with confidence and peace here and now. We do not need to worry about evil gaining the upper hand, but can resist evil and the forces of darkness in our world in the knowledge that their days are numbered. This is perhaps the most powerful part of the good news you and I can proclaim. There is hope. Trust in Christ. Unite your life to him, for he is the one guaranteed to triumph.

The scriptures are clear about this coming Kingdom. Some powerful passages include:

Matthew 13:31-33: He told them another parable: "The kingdom of heaven is like a mustard seed, which a man took and planted in his field. Though it is the smallest of all your seeds, yet when it grows, it is the largest of garden plants and becomes a tree, so that the birds of the air come and perch in its branches." He told them still another parable: "The kingdom of heaven is like yeast that a woman took and mixed into a large amount of flour until it worked all through the dough."

Matthew 25:31-46: "When the Son of Man comes in his glory, and all the angels with him, he will sit on his throne in heavenly glory. All the nations will be gathered before him, and he will separate the people one from another as a shepherd separates the sheep from the goats. He will put the sheep on his right and the goats on his left. Then the King will say to those on his right, 'Come, you who are blessed by my Father; take your inheritance, the kingdom prepared for you since the creation of the world. For I was hungry and you gave me something to eat, I was thirsty and you gave me something to drink, I was a stranger and you invited me in, I needed clothes and you clothed me, I was sick and you looked after me, I was in prison and you came to visit me.' Then the righteous will answer him, 'Lord, when did we see you hungry and feed you, or thirsty and give you something to drink? When did we see you a stranger and invite you in, or needing clothes and clothe you? When did we see you sick or in prison and go to visit you?' The King will reply, 'I tell you the truth, whatever you did for one of the least of these brothers of mine, you did for me.'

Then he will say to those on his left, 'Depart from me, you who are cursed, into the eternal fire prepared for the devil and his angels. For I was hungry and you gave me nothing to eat, I was thirsty and you gave me nothing to drink, I was a stranger and you did not invite me in, I needed clothes and you did not clothe me, I was sick and in prison and you did not look after me.' They also will answer, 'Lord, when did we see you hungry or thirsty or a stranger or needing clothes or sick or in prison, and did not help you?' He will reply, 'I tell you the truth, whatever you did not do for one of the least of these, you did not do for me.' Then they will go away to eternal punishment, but the righteous to eternal life."

Romans 6:23: For the wages of sin is death, but the gift of God is eternal life in Christ Jesus our Lord.

1 Thessalonians 4:16-18: For the Lord himself will come down from heaven, with a loud command, with the voice of the archangel and with the trumpet call of God, and the dead in Christ will rise first. After that, we who are still alive and are left will be caught up together with them in the clouds to meet the Lord in the air. And so we will be with the Lord forever. Therefore encourage each other with these words.

Revelation 21:1-4: Then I saw a new heaven and a new earth, for the first heaven and the first earth had passed away, and there was no longer any sea. I saw the Holy City, the new Jerusalem, coming down out of heaven from God, prepared as a bride beautifully dressed for her husband. And I heard a loud voice from the throne saying, "Now the dwelling of God is with men, and he will live with them. They will be his people, and God himself will be with them and be their God. He will wipe every tear from their eyes. There will be no more death or mourning or crying or pain, for the old order of things has passed away."

THINK ABOUT IT
Today's "Building Block" is: **God's Kingdom Is Coming**. Write in your own words what this means to you.

Envision some of the interactions and conversations you have in a typical week. What are some occasions when you might be able to share a little good news by mentioning your belief that God's kingdom is coming?
- A discussion about the injustice in our world could lead you to talk about the day when justice will come once and for all.
- A discussion about the rich getting richer and the poor seeming to get poorer might lead you to mention that one day there will be a great reversal.
-
-

61

-
-

TRY IT OUT

Take out your index card and write the number 6 and today's building block. Look at your card throughout the day and remind yourself of this key building block.

Keep alert today for opportunities you might have to talk about the fact that God's Kingdom is coming. Offer this bit of good news when appropriate opportunities present themselves.

DAY SEVEN: *The Good News Calls for a Response*

The good news of Jesus Christ is a message that demands a response. The message is so powerful, so hopeful, so challenging, and so life-changing, that one cannot be confronted without responding in some way.

Responses to the good news will vary. Not everyone responds in a positive manner. Not everyone will embrace the good news. When the Jewish leaders of Jesus' time were confronted by good news in the person of Jesus himself, they put Jesus to death on the cross. The story of Jesus' encounter with a rich young ruler ends with an unclear response. After Jesus calls the man to break his addiction to riches by giving all he has to the poor, we are told that the man turns and goes on his way. We cannot expect that every time we share good news we will have a positive response.

Sometimes the good news offends and calls for dramatic change. The good news may call for some to stop oppressive practices. It may call for some to give up their wealth. Good news may challenge people to break out of their isolation and reach out to others who are different from them. Good news may sometimes be hard to hear, and some persons may not be ready or willing to hear it. Thus, they may reject the good news, at least for the present.
However, when the good news is shared and received, it can produce powerful, life-changing results. Some refer to this as being "born again," a term that comes from the story of Nicodemus in the Gospel of John. Some may refer to this as "receiving salvation" or "being saved." Others may call it "professing your faith" or "becoming a disciple" or "repenting and coming to God." The terminology is not important. What is important is that the good news evokes a response that changes lives and brings persons back into fellowship with God.

The response to the good news may be demonstrated in numerous ways. One person may join the church. Another may respond by making a commitment to give a percentage of their income to the church and make a financial sacrifice. Yet another may embark on a life of committed discipleship, looking for ways to serve Christ through acts of devotion, worship, compassion, and justice. Someone else may fall on his knees and confess his sin and seek God's forgiveness and help. Some persons will choose baptism or renewal of their baptism as ways to respond to this good news.

The bottom line is that when God becomes a man and dies on a cross and rises from the dead, and promises to come again, we cannot just go on living as if it is business as usual. The world is different because of what God has done. And when we hear this good news, we need to respond.

A later session talks about inviting response and some of the ways to do that. This building block serves to remind us to invite response. After having presented the gospel or discussing spiritual things with another, give the other the opportunity to respond. Ask, "What do you now say about this?" "What is your response?" You aren't trying to close a deal or make a sale. You are simply inviting another to respond to the most dramatic good news that has ever happened. To engage in dialogue about Christ without inviting a response can leave a person hanging, wanting to do more, knowing hi or she is led to do more, but not sure what happens next.

Naturally you don't invite response every time you mention Christ or share a bit of the good news. Pray for the Holy Spirit's guidance about when it is appropriate to invite response. An invitation to respond to the good news is most often appropriate in relationships that have been cultivated and deepened or at times when there has been serious in-depth discussion about the good news that has been shared.

Some scriptures that show persons responding to the good news include:

Matthew 4:18-22: As Jesus was walking beside the Sea of Galilee, he saw two brothers, Simon called Peter and his brother Andrew. They were casting a net into the lake, for they were fishermen. "Come, follow me," Jesus said, "and I will make you fishers of men." At once they left their nets and followed him. Going on from there, he saw two other brothers, James son of Zebedee and his brother John. They were in a boat with their father Zebedee, preparing their nets. Jesus called them, and immediately they left the boat and their father and followed him.

Luke 19:1-10: Jesus entered Jericho and was passing through. A man was there by the name of Zacchaeus; he was a chief tax collector and was wealthy. He wanted to see who Jesus was, but being a short man he could not, because of the crowd. So he ran ahead and climbed a sycamore-fig tree to see him, since Jesus was coming that way. When Jesus reached the spot, he looked up and said to him, "Zacchaeus, come down immediately. I must stay at your house today." So he came down at once and welcomed him gladly. All the people saw this and began to mutter, "He has gone to be the guest of a 'sinner.' " But Zacchaeus stood up and said to the Lord, "Look, Lord! Here and now I give half of my possessions to the poor, and if I have cheated anybody out of anything, I will pay back four times the amount." Jesus said to him, "Today salvation has come to this house, because this man, too, is a son of Abraham. For the Son of Man came to seek and to save what was lost."

John 3:1-8: Now there was a man of the Pharisees named Nicodemus, a member of the Jewish ruling council. He came to Jesus at night and said, "Rabbi, we know you are a teacher who has come from God. For no one could perform the miraculous signs you are doing if God were not with him." In reply Jesus declared, "I tell you the truth, no one can see the kingdom of God unless he is born again." "How can a man be born when he is old?" Nicodemus asked. "Surely he cannot enter a second time into his mother's womb to be born!" Jesus answered, "I tell you the truth, no one can enter the kingdom of God unless he is born of water and the Spirit. Flesh gives birth to flesh, but the Spirit gives birth to spirit. You should not be surprised at my saying, 'You must be born again.' The wind blows wherever it pleases. You hear its sound, but you cannot tell where it comes from or where it is going. So it is with everyone born of the Spirit."

Romans 8:1-4: Therefore, there is now no condemnation for those who are in Christ Jesus, because through Christ Jesus the law of the Spirit of life set me free from the law of sin and death. For what the law was powerless to do in that it was weakened by the sinful nature, God did by sending his own Son in the likeness of sinful man to be a sin offering. And so he condemned sin in sinful man, in order that the righteous requirements of the law might be fully met in us, who do not live according to the sinful nature but according to the Spirit.

Ephesians 2:1-5: As for you, you were dead in your transgressions and sins, in which you used to live when you followed the ways of this world and of the ruler of the kingdom of the air, the spirit who is now at work in those who are disobedient. All of us also lived among them at one time, gratifying the cravings of our sinful nature and following its desires and thoughts. Like the rest, we were by nature objects of wrath. But because of his great love for us, God, who is rich in mercy, made us alive with Christ even when we were dead in transgressions-it is by grace you have been saved.

John 1:10-13: He was in the world, and though the world was made through him, the world did not recognize him. He came to that which was his own, but his own did not receive him. Yet to all who received him, to those who believed in his name, he gave the right to become children of God-children born not of natural descent, nor of human decision or a husband's will, but born of God.

THINK ABOUT IT

Today's "Building Block" is: **The Good News Calls for a Response**. Write in your own words what that means to you.

Envision some of the interactions and conversations you have in a typical week. What are some occasions when you might be able to share a little good news and then invite a response?

- After talking with someone about the birth of his or her child you share a little about the goodness of creation and a God who creates. You invite response by asking if you can share together in a prayer of thanksgiving and praise.
- You have begun to talk more and more about the good news with a friend at work. She expresses increasing interest. One day you ask, "Would you like to commit your life to Christ and become a disciple?"
-
-
-

TRY IT OUT

Take out your index card and write the number 7 and today's building block. Look at your card throughout the day and remind yourself of all seven building blocks that you have listed. Save this card and carry it with you throughout the remainder of this study. Use it to remind you of the essential building blocks of the good news message.

Keep alert today for opportunities you might have to invite a response to the good news.

SUMMARY OF WEEK THREE:

THE BUILDING BLOCKS OF THE GOSPEL

A Good God Created a Good Creation
Humans Sin; Creation Is Broken
Jesus of Nazareth
Jesus Dies on a Cross
Jesus Was Raised on the Third Day
God's Kingdom Is Coming
The Good News Calls for a Response

These Building Blocks are reproduced on the last regular page of this study guide. At the end of the course, you may want to cut it out and carry it in your purse, pocket, or wallet for future reference.

GROUP MEETING FOR WEEK 3

Praying together

Review of this week's material

Exercises, role plays, or case studies

As a large group share some of the ways each of the building blocks might be used in daily interactions. Look back over the "Think About It" sections where students have pondered this during the past week. Compile the list on the board or on newsprint. Divide into groups of two or three. Have each small group select two of the scenarios from the list and role play the situation. If time permits and members are willing, have some of the small groups share their role plays with the entire class.

Telling our story

Leader Input
There are still two Great Commission passages we have not yet examined. In earlier sessions, we looked at the passages from John and Matthew. Great Commissions are also included in Mark and Luke. These passages form the mandate...the command of Jesus that we do the work of evangelism.

Today your group will look at the two remaining passages. Divide your class into two smaller groups. Assign one to look at Mark 16:15 (14-20 if they want to look at this verse in its entire context). Assign the other group to look at Luke 24:44-49.

Invite the groups to look at the passages and ask the following questions:

What did this passage say to its original audience?
What does this passage say to the church today?
What does this passage say to me as an individual?

Give the groups some time to process these questions and then ask them to report their findings. You will want to be sure to note the following observations about the passages:

Mark:
- Jesus' simple command is to "Go!"
- Evangelism means to "Proclaim."
- The content of evangelism is the "Good News."

Luke:
- Evangelism involves the proclamation of repentance and forgiveness.
- This work begins locally (in Jerusalem) and expands to the whole world (all nations).
- The Spirit empowers disciples to do this work.

As you look at these passages, emphasize once again that evangelism is a mandate from Jesus. He gives this as a challenge and command. A Great Commission is present in each of the gospels. You may even want to take a few moments to review the other Great Commissions you have already studied. The Great Commission passages are:

Matthew 28:16-20
Mark 16:14-10 (especially verse 15)
Luke 24:44-49
John 20:19-23

Assignments
> **Visits to prospects, shut-ins**
> **Telling our story next week**
> **Testimonies at worship**

Closing prayer time

Evaluation

OPPORTUNITIES TO TELL THE STORY

DAY ONE: *Evangelism Is Hospitality*

Let mutual love continue. Do not neglect to show hospitality to strangers, for by doing that some have entertained angels without knowing it.
Hebrews 13:1-2 (NRSV)

On one occasion when Jesus was going to the house of a leader of the Pharisees to eat a meal on the Sabbath, they were watching him closely.

When he noticed how the guests chose the places of honor, he told them a parable. "When you are invited by someone to a wedding banquet, do not sit down at the place of honor, in case someone more distinguished than you has been invited by your host; and those who invited both of you may come and say to you, 'Give this person your place,' and then in disgrace you would start to take the lowest place. But when you are invited, go and sit down at the lowest place, so that when your host comes, he may say to you, 'Friend, move up higher;' then you will be honored in the presence of all who sit at the table with you. For all who exalt themselves will be humbled, and those who humble themselves will be exalted."

He said also to the one who had invited him, "When you give a luncheon or a dinner, do not invite your friends or your brothers or your relatives or rich neighbors, in case they may invite you in return, and you would be repaid. But when you give a banquet, invite the poor, the crippled, the lame, and the blind. And you will blessed, because they cannot repay you, for you will be repaid at the resurrection of the righteous.
Luke 14:1, 7-14 (NRSV)

When you look at the Bible, a theme that keeps appearing is the theme of hospitality. The writer of Hebrews calls on his readers to practice hospitality, for in doing so, many have entertained angels without knowing it.

Jesus tells his host at a great banquet to make a place for the poor, the downtrodden, the crippled, and those who are less fortunate. He is talking about hospitality. His vision is a banquet where all are made to be welcome, a place where all are accepted.

The familiar story of the woman at the well is another hospitality story. Jesus meets the woman where she is. He doesn't judge her, but acknowledges her troubled, unhappy life, and then offers her living water to drink (John 4:7-26). He is the host, offering refreshment for the parched soul.

Have you ever considered that your evangelism is simply hospitality? You welcome others to God's table. You share good news with those who hunger and thirst. You stand at the door as a greeter for God's Kingdom. Talking about Jesus and doing evangelism is to show hospitality on God's behalf. It is a gracious act. It is a compassionate act. It is done with love and care and concern.

THINK ABOUT IT
Have you ever thought about evangelism being a form of hospitality?

How does such a model of evangelism make you feel about doing the work of evangelism?

How can you be a better host or hostess at God's table?

TRY IT OUT
During the day today, keep your eyes open for persons who are showing hospitality. Where are they? How are they acting? How can such hospitality be put to work for God?

DAY TWO: *More on Hospitality*

K-Mart is having a rough time getting off the ground in the former Communist Czech Republic. Back in 1992, K-Mart acquired a chain of department stores there...but it seems as though the clerks know nothing about customer service. Back in the old days, under communist rule, you didn't need to know anything about customer service. There was no such thing. But now things have changed. Under a free-market society, customer service is the norm. Customer service is expected. But K-Mart officials are having a hard time convincing their communist-trained clerks that they should provide service to the customer. The clerks do not even want to be friendly to the customer.

One woman clerk says, "It was easy before. We were just sitting behind the counter and customers came to us. Now we have to walk around and go to the customers. My feet hurt." In the old days sales clerks were tyrants. They despised the shoppers and the shoppers despised them. Clerks dismissed customer inquiries with a shout or a shrug. A customer would never dare to interrupt a clerk who was chatting with a fellow worker or talking on the phone to a friend. No one wanted to incur the wrath of an angry sales clerk.

And now along comes K-Mart. Their slogan is "customers first" and workers are required to wear a badge that says, "I am here for you." The workers are angry and humiliated. K-Mart has a major re-education job ahead of them as they try to teach the Czech workers something about customer service.

Really, what we are talking about here is a very basic thing called hospitality. You and I expect hospitality everywhere we go, whether it is K-Mart, McDonald's, or the local grocery store. When we don't experience hospitality, we are upset and complain to the management.

Hospitality is no less important when it comes to sharing the good news of Jesus Christ. In fact, hospitality is more important, because the good news is about hospitality. God welcomes God's people into relationship. God welcomes us to God's table. The good news is that God shows hospitality.

Our task is to show a bit of God's hospitality to a world where too few experience hospitality. Many of those around us have been hurt, rebuked, cut off, and estranged in their relationships with others in the world. They do not feel welcomed or accepted. Hospitality and grace have not been made real in their lives. As evangelists, our task is to offer a little good news, a little hospitality, and a little grace in a world that denies the importance of these things.

Are you intimidated about talking about Jesus? Are you afraid of being perceived as pushy, or coming on too strong? Are you worried that talking about Jesus will make you something of an intruder into places where you are not welcome?

Perhaps what is called for is a different view of evangelism. Instead of viewing your evangelistic attempts as intrusive invasions of other's privacy, look at them as a means of showing hospitality. You are offering others a bit of grace. You are extending a hand of love. You are giving words of life. You are offering God's best with hospitality and warmth and grace.

THINK ABOUT IT
What are some characteristics of hospitality?

What normally turns you off about people who do evangelism?

Do you think they are evangelizing out of a model of hospitality?

What would be different if hospitality were at the root of all evangelism?

How does your church offer hospitality to the "stranger" in its midst?

What could your church do better? How can you contribute to that effort?

TRY IT OUT
Spend some time today talking with a friend, family member, or co-worker about the idea of hospitality as the basis of evangelism. How does he/she react to this concept? Is this a new idea to him/her?

DAY THREE: *Life's Transition Times*

In an earlier lesson, we talked about the parable of the sower as a good model of evangelism. The sower sows the seed, knowing full well that some of it will land on stones, or among the weeds, or be eaten by the birds. However, there is the hope and potential that some of the seed will land on soil that is ready to receive the seed, and the seed will put down roots and develop into strong healthy plants. Likewise, while some of our gospel efforts will be ineffective as they fall on deaf, unreceptive ears, some of the good news will be heard by people who are open, receptive, and ready to respond in a positive, life-changing way. When we have the opportunity to share good news with those who are prepared to receive the gospel message, it is important that we share it in ways that connect with them where they are.

How do we know when persons are at those points in life when they are ready to hear and receive God's good news? One indicator that persons are open to a deeper spiritual experience is when they are facing those times in life that can be called "transition times." Transition times are those times that we all face sooner or later. During transition times, we often pause and reflect on the direction we are headed. We rethink our priorities and values. We make changes and, we hope, move forward in positive ways that make for wholeness and healing. Sometimes, persons get stuck in transition times and do not do the work they need to do to move ahead, and the transition becomes a burden they carry the rest of their lives.

During transition times, when persons are thinking, rethinking, and seeking, they are often more open to talking about and looking at things of the spirit. Transition times are excellent opportunities to talk with others about Jesus and offer his good news, healing, and wholeness. These are times when persons will really appreciate and respond to good news that is offered with a sense of hospitality.

Some of life's transition times might include:
- leaving home
- starting a job or changing jobs
- being laid off or fired
- getting married
- having the first child; having additional children
- illness or death of a spouse
- the breakup of a marriage
- the breakup of a significant relationship
- moving to a new place
- retirement and the empty nest
- a serious illness
- miscarriage or stillbirth
- the illness or death of a child
- a life-changing accident
- legal or financial problems
- illness, disability, or death of one's parents

During transition times, people are seeking. They need hope, they need assurance, they need something to hold on to, they are looking for direction. They may express questions about the meaning of life or whether it is all worth it. They may wonder about the reality of God or why bad things happen to good people. These are indicators that the person is opening up to talk about some of life's deeper questions and experiences.

When a friend, family member, or co-worker faces a transition time or indicates that he or she is wrestling with some profound questions, don't just smile and walk away. Instead, a light should go off in your mind as you think, "This is a time to offer the hope and good news of Jesus." Then stop, listen to your friend, express your concern and desire to understand, and try to connect with your friend at his or her point of deepest need. Be sure to pray for the direction of God's spirit that you can respond in ways that are helpful, appropriate, and offer good news.

We will look at some of those specific responses in future sessions.

THINK ABOUT IT
What transition times can you add to the above list?

Can you think of a transition time in your life when you grew spiritually and moved closer to God?

Have you seen others make significant changes in their relationship to God as a result of passing through a transition time?

Have you ever spoken to someone about the hope of Jesus Christ during a transition time?

Persons who are seeking something more often couch their need in key questions or veiled statements. Make a list of some of these statements and questions and try to train yourself to be ready to enter into deeper conversation when you hear these.
Examples: "Is this all there is to life?" "I want my life to count." "Is there purpose to my life?" etc.
-
-
-
-
-
-
-
-

TRY IT OUT

This week you have been observing, listening, and developing skills in determining when persons might be open to hearing the good news. By now, you have discovered some persons in your workplace, family, or community who are facing transition times, searching for deeper meaning in life, or asking some forms of ultimate questions. List two or three of those persons here and write a little about how you might engage them in a discussion about Jesus Christ and his good news.

1.

2.

3.

DAYS FOUR AND FIVE: *Connecting Transition Times with the Building Blocks of the Gospel*

Last week we discussed the building blocks of the gospel message. These building blocks sum up the core of the good news Christ offers to the world.

Naturally, this good news can speak to those who are facing life's transition times. A person struggling with alcoholism might find hope in the knowledge of a Savior who has power to overcome the grave. Power to overcome the grave indicates a power that can overcome even alcoholism.

A person struggling with guilt may find comfort in the knowledge of a God who forgives sin. In fact, this God went so far as to sacrifice his son in an effort to demonstrate his willingness to confront and forgive sin.

These are connections between the building blocks of the gospel and the key events of life. It is helpful to consider each of these building blocks and to think about where it may intersect with some of life's situations. If we think about these connections in advance, we can be better prepared to offer a relevant bit of good news when we encounter those facing transition times.

This is a two day assignment. Spend time today and tomorrow working on making connections between the building blocks of the gospel and life's transition times.

THINK ABOUT IT

The building blocks of the gospel are listed below. Think about each one and consider what transition time it might effectively speak to. Use the list of transition times from day three and relate each one to a relevant portion of the gospel. Add your own transition times to the list as well.

BUILDING BLOCK: **TRANSITION TIMES:**

1. A Good God Created a Good Creation

2. Humans Sin; Creation Is Broken

3. Jesus of Nazareth

4. Jesus Dies on a Cross

5. Jesus Was Raised on the Third Day

6. God's Kingdom Is Coming

7. The Good News Calls for a Response

Now let's try it another way. In the exercise above, we gave you the Building Block and you came up with a transition time that it might address. Listed below are some transition times. As you read through them, try to come up with a Building Block that might speak to this specific situation. For example, a transition time of the birth of a child might provide an opening for you to speak about the goodness of God. Remember, this is a two day assignment. If you are struggling, call another member of the class and brainstorm it together.

TRANSITION TIME   **BUILDING BLOCK**

- leaving home

- starting a job or changing jobs

- being laid off or fired

- getting married

- having the first child; having additional children

- illness or death of a spouse

- the breakup of a marriage

- the breakup of a significant relationship

- moving to a new place

- retirement and the empty nest

TRY IT OUT

Today it is likely that you will encounter someone facing one of life's transition times. Consider two of those situations in this space. Write a little bit about the situation and how one or more of the building blocks connect with that situation.

Situation 1:

How the building blocks of the gospel connect with the situation:

Situation 2:

How the building blocks of the gospel connect with the situation:

Can you enter into conversation in any of these situations and talk with the person about the way the good news might intersect with his or her life? Give it a try.

DAY SIX: *Telling Your Story*

The man had been blind from birth. Life must have been hard for him. He couldn't hold a job. He was dependent on others to support him and care for him. Most likely, he was reduced to begging along the side of the road.

Then he had an encounter that changed his life. He met Jesus Christ. Jesus spat on the ground, made mud with the saliva, and spread the mud on the man's eyes. Following Jesus' command, the man washed in the pool of Siloam and he was able to see. His neighbors were, naturally, curious about this sudden change. One who had been blind from birth could now see and they wondered what had happened. They asked him, "How were your eyes opened?" The man responded by telling his story: "The man called Jesus made mud, spread it on my eyes, and said to me, 'Go to Siloam and wash.' Then I went and washed and received my sight."

The account, as recorded in John 9 (NRSV), continues as others question the man about his newly found sight. The Pharisees wonder what happened. His parents are brought in and are questioned about this miracle. When he is asked by the Pharisees a second time, he answers, "Here is an astonishing thing! You do not know where he comes from, and yet he opened my eyes. We know that God does not listen to sinners, but he does listen to one who worships him and obeys his will. Never since the world began has it been heard that anyone opened the eyes of a person born blind. If this man were not from God, he could do nothing."

This story is not just a story about a healing. It is a model for our own evangelism and faith sharing. A man who has been touched and changed by Jesus tells his story to those who will listen to him. Story telling is a valid, effective model for talking about Jesus.

In years past, the church made a place for story telling. It was called giving a testimony. Worship services often included opportunities for persons to give testimonies and tell their stories of what Jesus has meant to them and done in their lives. For some reason, the modern church has lost this tradition. Perhaps it is a tradition that needs to be recovered.

In my own congregation, we experimented with sharing testimonies a few years ago during a capital funds campaign. For six weeks leading up to the time we received giving commitments, various members of the congregation shared a five-minute testimony during the worship service. Some of the stories were profound, while most were simple expressions of average people and their encounters with Christ. All were moving. Those services stand out in the memories of many persons because good news was shared by telling our own personal stories.

You have a story to tell. It may be as profound as the healing of the man born blind. Perhaps God has done something dramatic in your life-a healing or something miraculous.

Most likely, your story is not so dramatic. Perhaps it is a story of a time when God was present with you through a personal struggle. Maybe your story is a time when a relationship was restored and forgiveness was experienced. Your story could be a time when you experienced Jesus as you reached out to one who was hurting or needy. Very often our stories come from one of our own transition times when we experienced Christ in a new and deeper way.

Telling our stories is an effective form of evangelism. By telling your story, you tell another what Christ means in your life and share the good news that he is alive and real to you.

What we need to do, however, is to get in touch with our stories. Some thought needs to go into them, so when the opportunity for sharing comes, we are prepared to share. Today and tomorrow we will do some work on our own personal stories. The goal is not to come up with a prepared, scripted, canned approach to sharing the faith. Instead our goal is for each of us to be in touch with our own stories so that they will flow naturally when the opportunity to share is presented.

THINK ABOUT IT

As we get in touch with our stories, it is helpful to think through our own spiritual journeys. Today's questions will help you in that process.

When did you first come to an awareness of Jesus Christ in your life?

What are one or two times that Jesus Christ has been especially real to you?

Are there times when you felt that God was far away? How did God break through so you experienced his closeness once again?

When has Christ strengthened you and walked with you through a challenging time?

When has Christ come to you as you reached out in service to others?

Are there particular building blocks of the gospel that have spoken to you in an especially meaningful way?

TRY IT OUT

Take some time today to read the full story of the man born blind. It is found in John 9.

Continue to work on yesterday's assignments where you connect building blocks with life's transition times.

DAY SEVEN: *Telling Your Story, Part Two*

Yesterday you considered your own personal faith story. The questions to think about provided a chance to examine your faith journey and to see some of those points where Jesus Christ was most real.

Today we are going to ask you actually to write out your faith story. Remember, this doesn't have to be a full blown history of your life. It can be a particular event. It might be a time period that you went through. It might just be an occasion when you came to a sense of peace or a deeper awareness of Jesus in your life.

Often we think that our faith stories have to be dramatic or profound. We hear of the people who turned from drug addicts to disciples through the power of Jesus Christ and feel somehow inadequate if our stories aren't that dramatic. However, most stories are not that kind of dramatic turnaround. Most of the time, God's grace works in our lives and touches us in more quiet, intimate, less dramatic ways. Keep that in mind as you write your story today. Also, look for ways you have been touched by the building blocks of the gospel in your own experience. If you can, include these in your story.

Today's work may take more than ten or fifteen minutes. If you cannot complete the assignment now, feel free to begin, put it aside, and return to it again later in the day.

Use the space below for notes and then use the following page to write your story.

THINK ABOUT IT

My faith story:

TRY IT OUT
Find one or two opportunities to share your story with a friend or family member today.

GROUP MEETING FOR WEEK 4

Praying together

Review of this week's material

Exercises, role plays, or case studies
Divide the group into pairs. Assign each pair one of the situations listed below. Develop a dialogue between a person who is facing the given situation and the Christian attempting to offer the good news. Try to use one or more of the gospel building blocks that may be relevant to the situation.

> ### Situations:
> Suffered a miscarriage
> Lost a job
> Just got married
> Just had a child
> Learned you have a terminal disease
> Just visited the church for the first time
> Just survived a serious car accident
> Celebrated a 40th wedding anniversary
> Placed a parent in a nursing home

Telling our story

Leader Input

Some of the indicators of receptivity
During the past week we looked at some of life's transition times and the importance of being attuned to those times as opportunities for sharing the good news. Dr. George Hunter, a United Methodist minister and professor of evangelism, offers some other general indicators that may help us to realize when persons are facing transition times or are open to the gospel message. Hunter's indicators[15] are:

1. *Dissatisfaction:* When persons are dissatisfied with themselves and their lives, they are frequently open to the gospel. The good news may be what they are longing for to address their nagging questions, doubts, and concerns. Dissatisfaction with life may be connected with one of the transition times we discussed this past week.

---

[15]George G. Hunter, III, Contagious Congregations (Nashville: Abingdon, 1979), 113-115.

2. *Cultural Change:* Times of cultural change may produce an openness to hear the good news of Jesus Christ. Economic fluctuations, political upheaval, shifting cultural values, changing family structures, and disruptions in that which is familiar and comfortable may force persons to ponder their priorities and consider the issues of the spirit. Cultural change may be an important indicator that persons are ready to hear good news in the 1990s.

3. *Individual Stress:* This relates again to the transition times of last week's sessions. Transition times are usually times of increased stress. Symptoms of stress may vary. Keeping alert to such symptoms may provide openings to talk about Jesus Christ.

4. *The Masses:* Hunter writes, "In general, the church will usually find 'the masses' to be more responsive than 'the classes.' Missionary strategy has often been very wrong in emphasizing outreach first to the classes and only later to the masses."[16] Remember John Wesley's success in reaching the masses of 18th century England. His outreach to the masses sparked a revival that led to the creation of the Methodist Church.

5. *Growing Religions:* A person who is seeking Jesus Christ may turn to other religious faiths and experiences to meet his or her spiritual hunger. Thus, when one talks about exploring other religious practices and experimenting with alternative belief systems, that person may be open to talking about Jesus. Hunter writes, "Christians should not presuppose that a growing non-Christian religion is actually fulfilling peoples' needs-it may only be engaging their needs in ways that will later prove unfulfilling-analogous to a thirsty man's drinking salty ocean water and engaging his thirst but not satisfying it."[17]

Do not view remarks about exploring other religions as an end to conversation. Instead, use such remarks as opportunities to explore the questions and concerns that are leading the person to seek answers in the other religion. You may find opportunities during the discussion to offer good news and suggest that Jesus can feed the spiritual hunger she is experiencing.

Assignments
> **Visits to prospects, shut-ins**
> **Telling our story next week**
> **Testimonies at worship**

Closing prayer time

Evaluation

---

[16]Ibid., 114.
[17]Ibid., 115.

SOME FINAL ESSENTIALS

DAY ONE: *Some Basic Principles*

So far, we have discussed and examined a wide range of evangelism philosophy as well as a number of practical suggestions. Today, I want to share a few key principles as you continue your ministry of evangelism.

1. **Begin with prayer.** The foundation of our ministry of evangelism must be a foundation of prayer. This includes regular prayer as part of your daily devotional life. It also includes prayer before, during, and after your faith-sharing encounters. As I approach the home and ring the doorbell of someone I am going to visit, I normally breathe a silent prayer that God will be present and guide the encounter. While we are together, I try to offer a brief silent prayer that I will respond appropriately, especially if a problem or concern is being shared. Finally, as I leave the encounter, I will pray silently that God will use what has transpired to God's glory.

2. **Understand the reason you are doing this work.** We have discussed the purpose of evangelism numerous times throughout this course. Remember that, as an evangelist, your purpose is not to change another person to your way of thinking. Your purpose is to offer the love of Christ. You are offering a bit of good news. Any conversion or transformation is God's work. You are not in charge of getting anyone saved or converted. You are simply sharing the unconditional grace offered by our God.

3. **Be a good listener.** Too often we think that evangelizing involves talking, selling, convincing, or imposing. I would suggest that a far better activity than any of these is listening. Listen and try to really hear where a person is coming from. Listen to the person's concerns. Listen for what is important in this person's life. As you listen, you demonstrate a true interest in this person and you build up a relationship of trust. Listening is a way of caring, a way of showing grace, and it earns you the right to be heard.

4. **Many times the most significant sharing occurs in the final moments of an encounter.** I can recall many instances when I have been visiting a church friend at home or in the hospital. The visit has proceeded well, but without any in-depth sharing. When I think it is time to conclude the visit, I say "good-bye," perhaps pray, and then prepare to

leave. Just as I am getting up or opening the door, the person I have been visiting makes a seemingly offhand comment, or says, "Just one more thing." This is often a moment of opportunity. Many times, this is when an individual brings up a concern or question that is really on his or her heart. Perhaps he or she was holding it in throughout the visit and now finds that this is the last chance to mention it. These last minute conversations are often the door we have been looking for to share the good news of Christ. Keep alert for what is going on at the end of the visit.

5. **Keep your eyes and ears open to signs that come from the person's environment.** Suppose that you have dropped by to see someone who has visited your church. You think this is an opportunity to share the good news of Jesus and perhaps engage in some evangelism. As you go into the home, you see pictures of babies on the mantle, a wheelchair tucked away in the kitchen corner, and a piano in the living room. You could look at these things and think nothing of them. Or, you could let these items be signals of what is important in the life of this family. The baby pictures could indicate children or grandchildren. The wheelchair could indicate a handicapped person in the household, or perhaps someone recovering from hospitalization. The piano lets you know that perhaps this family is interested in music, popular music, or sacred music perhaps. Observe these signals and respond to them as you enter into conversation. By taking seriously the clues from a person's world, you begin to know where to start in a conversation. You can be interested in what they are interested in. Your interest might even open the way to a deeply spiritual conversation. Perhaps this family has been thinking about the significance of having those babies baptized. Or maybe the person in the wheelchair is an elderly parent who needs special care, and the caregiver is on the verge of exhaustion because of the demands. Either of these situations provides an opportunity to engage in spiritual conversation and a sharing of Jesus Christ.

The key is to observe the environment, and then to respond in a grace-ful, caring manner. Harry Denman, the beloved Methodist evangelist, was a master at this kind of observation and response. He even suggested paying attention to the furniture, especially old furniture. He once said, "Remember, behind every old piece of furniture there is a family story." When we show an interest in such family stories, we open the way to share the gospel of Jesus Christ.

6. **People sometimes offer bits of information that invite us to engage in deeper conversation.** Often times persons will make a statement that dangles just a bit of information before us. Examples include statements like "I've been having some health problems lately." Or, "I just don't know what to do about that daughter of mine." These bits of information are invitations to us to pursue the conversation and go deeper into the relationship. If we respond appropriately and invite them to tell us more, they will. And we will find ourselves dealing with the other's deepest hurts and hopes and will have opportunities to share the good news and grace of Jesus. On the other hand, we can choose not to respond, nod our head thoughtfully, change the subject, and miss out on an opportunity to talk about Jesus.

7. **Be willing to be vulnerable.** Vulnerability indicates a capability of being hurt or open to pain. Jesus himself demonstrated vulnerability. He was vulnerable enough to be put to death on a cross. Perhaps Jesus' vulnerability is an example to those of us who follow him to be willing to be vulnerable ourselves. We can say "I don't know." We can shed tears with the other. We can admit that we don't have all the answers, that we, too, are seekers. Witnessing for Jesus doesn't mean we are invulnerable experts. An effective witness sometimes stammers, cries, hurts, and lets his or her guard down. By being vulnerable we share God's love as Jesus himself shared God's love.

8. **Evangelism is not trying to change another person.** Evangelism is simply telling why and in whom I believe. Talking about Jesus is not convincing, arguing, or offering lots of scripture passages. It is simply sharing our story of what and why we believe, and allowing others to see through our story how Christ can have an impact upon their story.

THINK ABOUT IT
Are there principles you would add to the list?

Which principle seems most important to you?

What are some ways you can take seriously another's surroundings?

Try to imagine a conversation in which a person volunteers a bit of information as an invitation to pursue the conversation a bit further. Write a couple of those invitational statements in this space:

TRY IT OUT

This week, try to make a visit to a prospective church member. Get a name from the pastor, get in touch with the person or family, and set up a time to call in the home. Keep these principles in mind as you go out on behalf of Christ and your church.

DAY TWO: *The Realities: Attitude, Ability, Opportunity, and Mandate*

We have spent several weeks now looking at various aspects of evangelism. Today and tomorrow, I want us to consider some reasons Christians don't engage in more evangelism. I do not suggest these as conclusive reasons we hesitate to engage in evangelism. I do not even profess to have done a scientific study of the issue. However, I do propose that there are four significant reasons that many of us shy away from evangelism. I base these suggestions upon studies, surveys, and interviews conducted in a church with which I am familiar.

Based upon the responses to my research, I discovered that reasons for a lack of involvement in evangelism can be classified into four categories:

1. Attitudes about evangelism.
2. Lack of or perceived lack of ability to evangelize.
3. Little or no opportunity to do evangelism.
4. Little or no sense of a mandate to evangelize.

These four categories- attitude, ability, opportunity, and mandate- point to some significant reasons we do not engage in as much evangelism as we probably could or should. We will look at each of these in turn, two today, and two tomorrow.

Attitude: By far, the biggest hindrance to evangelism among the people I surveyed is their attitude or understanding of evangelism. There is a sense that evangelism is intrusive and unwelcome. Evangelistic Christians are perceived as obnoxious, pushy, invasive people who overstep the bounds of privacy. The Christians I talked to do not want to come across in this manner. They do not see themselves forcing the gospel on their friends or pushing scripture verses on their co-workers. Because they understand evangelism to be this kind of activity, they avoid it rather than attempt to share the good news in ways that are more tasteful and gentle, and actually, more in keeping with the gospel that they seek to share. By not sharing at all, they avoid the sting of rejection. Some specific comments heard include:

> "I'm not afraid, except I don't want to make the mistake of trying to cram my religion down people's throats."
> "Some people feel you are 'pushing' your belief."
> "I don't want to get too involved in other people's business."

"I fear being a 'goody-goody' and judgment from others."
"I fear ridicule, rejection, and being labeled a 'fanatic.' "
"I don't want to risk offending someone because they don't believe as I do."
"I don't like others to impose their views on me, so I don't like to talk to others."
"I may turn someone off. They may think I'm interfering in their life."

These comments and many others like them point to an understanding that evangelism is somehow imposing one's belief system on others. If we are going to talk about our faith in Jesus Christ, it must be overbearing, pushy, inconsiderate, and confrontative. This understanding of evangelism contributes to the lack of faith-sharing by the people I encountered in my research.

Ability: The second category of response referred to the sense of a lack of ability to engage in evangelism. Some of those surveyed do not engage in sharing their good news about Jesus because they are unsure how to do it. They do not feel competent in terms of the doctrines of the church or the appropriate scriptures to quote, and thus they tend to avoid faith-related discussions altogether. Others simply view themselves as shy or introverted, and thus are not comfortable engaging in evangelism. Some of the comments related to lack of ability were:

"I'm not articulate about my faith."
"I have a fear of being 'cornered' and not having enough knowledge of the Bible to defend properly my beliefs on a given topic."
"I fear not representing God/Jesus well."
"Having it be appropriate to the person's particular circumstances."
"Saying the wrong thing, lack of knowledge."
"I would be somewhat unsure how to express my feelings."
"I have no memory for the proper verse."
"I am very shy."
"I'm not as informed as I'd like to be."

These responses seem to indicate that some persons are unsure of their abilities to engage in discussions about their faith. They have not memorized certain Bible passages, they are not totally sure of the arguments needed to defend their doctrine and beliefs, or they are not sure how to express what they believe. This lack of skill or ability in sharing the good news stifles their evangelism efforts and leads to few encounters where faith in Jesus is shared.

THINK ABOUT IT
Can you relate to attitude and ability as reasons that you do not share your faith more often?
How has this study addressed the issue of your attitudes about evangelism in a positive manner?

How has this study given you confidence in your abilities to engage in evangelism?

TRY IT OUT
Take your own informal survey. Does your evidence support the notion that attitude, ability, opportunity, and mandate are reasons persons do not engage in more ministries of evangelism?

DAY THREE: *Opportunity and Mandate*

<u>Opportunity</u>: Several of the people I talked with indicated that the reason they do not evangelize or share their faith in Jesus is because there is no opportunity for them to do so. Their responses sounded something like this:

> "I share only if something sparks a discussion and the other person acts interested."
> "There is hesitation when the opportunity comes up and I often miss the opening that was there."
> "I'm not reluctant to share my faith, it just doesn't come up often."
> "I just don't stop and think about it (the fast 90's lifestyles)."
> "It does not always seem 'appropriate,' especially in the workplace."
> "People have not been easy to talk to about this."

A lack of opportunity or perceived lack of opportunity seems to be a significant reason that some folks do not share their faith. Perhaps they do not recognize opportunities when they arise. Perhaps they are unsure what is an appropriate opportunity to talk about Jesus. In either case, some people believe that there is little or no opportunity to share their faith, and thus do not engage in evangelism.

Mandate: A foundational element in Christian evangelism is the fact that it is mandated by Christ himself. Christians are those who are sent to proclaim the good news. In Acts the commandment is given to go into the world, beginning with Jerusalem, and then into Judea, and finally to the ends of the earth. There is an urgency. There is a mandate. Evangelism is part of the call that comes with being a Christian.

Those with whom I talked in my research seem to have little or no sense of this mandate to evangelize. A good number seem to think that sharing the good news of Jesus is something they do among other Christians. Their faith-sharing happens as they gather with other Christians and affirm one another and build one another up in faith. These respondents lack a sense that sharing the good news of Jesus means going beyond our Christian friendships and calls for interacting with unbelievers in the world around us.

To their credit, some respondents indicated that they share as a response to what they have received. They know joy and peace and wholeness and salvation; they feel that they must offer that to others. By and large, however, the reasons for sharing are very subjective in nature. There is little sense of an objective call to share the good news of Jesus Christ. When asked why they share, some of the comments included:

> "I feel people need it. I want them to have the same joy I have."
> "It is a way to participate in Christian fellowship."
> "To let others share my beliefs."
> "Because I see so many troubled about life and faith."
> "To share the good news of God and Jesus Christ our Lord and Savior and the reassurance that brings."
> "I'm really concerned for them. Trying to help them solve problems in their life."
> "I would like others to know how great it is to know Jesus."
> "It is uplifting."
> "Because I feel as a Christian I should share."
> "I think faith is something everyone needs, especially in these times. I also think if another person sees in you a happiness and an outgoing attitude, it spills over to them and they show the same."
> "I share it with people because they might be interested also."
> "When you are saved and have Good News about eternal life, you want to tell others. Just like if we found a cure to cancer."

This is just a sampling of some of the responses people gave when asked why they share their faith. It is easy to notice the subjective nature of the responses. Very few of them express a sense of mandate, that this is something we do because Christ commands us to do it. It is almost as if sharing the good news is something optional that I do because it is fulfilling to me to do it. The lack of a clear mandate to share the good news of Christ is, perhaps, one of the reasons the good news is not shared more frequently by many Christians.

THINK ABOUT IT

Is a lack of opportunity a reason you do not engage in evangelism?

Do you believe that you are under a mandate by Christ to share your faith? Why or why not?

How has this course helped you better discern opportunities for evangelism?

How has this course developed your awareness of a mandate for evangelism?

Go back and look at the introductory session of this study. Four versions of The Great Commission are discussed there. Look each one up in your Bible and take some notes about how each one mandates us to share the gospel of Christ.

TRY IT OUT

Keep a list of evangelism opportunities that present themselves to you this week.

Talk with two or three other Christian friends about the mandate to do evangelism. Do they sense a mandate to do this work?

Call up someone from your study group or get together for a visit. Discuss together the mandates we are given in Matthew, Mark, Luke, and John. See the introductory session for specific references and information.

DAY FOUR: *Some Practical Suggestions*

Today we look at some some strategies that you can employ now as you reach out to persons with the gospel of Christ. The basis for these suggestions is Harold K. Bales' little booklet, Leading Persons to Christ.[18] These are practical strategies you can begin to use today.

Prayer. You can pray regularly for the persons you want to reach. This is powerful and helpful to them and to you. In addition, you can tell them you are praying for them. This is often a non-threatening response that is very much appreciated. If the circumstances allow, perhaps the most powerful response is to say "I think that prayer often makes a difference and that God hears our prayers. Could we just take a moment now and pray about your situation?" Then offer a brief prayer lifting the person's concerns up to God.

Conversation. Your words are a powerful witness. We will look more at conversation tomorrow.

Referral. You may refer a seeking person to another Christian who you believe will be able to help them. Such referrals may be made to your pastor, a teacher, or a lay person whom you trust and respect.

Invitation to a small group. Groups are places where we experience love, support, and encouragement. An invitation to Sunday School, Bible Study, United Methodist Men, etc. is a way to make a witness to Jesus Christ.

Invitation to worship. Inviting people to worship expresses your love and offers the chance for them to experience the Spirit moving among God's people. Most people visit worship and join a church because they have been invited by a caring friend.

---

[18]Harold K. Bales, Leading Persons to Christ (Kingsport, Tennessee: Precept, 1992), 21-24.

Natural social contact. You can talk about Jesus in those times and places where your paths naturally cross. School, work, the bus stop, or the hairdresser are such places.

Telephone calls. A caring telephone call can go a long way to making connection with those we care about and are seeking to reach. Calls are especially appreciated by persons struggling with loneliness and feelings of alienation. Perhaps an actual visit to the home is a real option here as well.

Letters. Short, hand-written notes carry a great witness. They can be read over and over again. The knowledge of the fact that you cared enough to take the time to write speaks volumes. Indicate that the recipient is in your thoughts and prayers and offer your love and encouragement.

The most effective witness is based on love, relationship, and caring that connects our life with the one we reach out to. Harold Bales tells of a young pastor who experienced a negative evangelism encounter as a youth at summer church camp. Another camper was determined to "get him saved." The minister said, "He hounded me from daylight 'til dark...Finally in sheer frustration I turned to him and asked, 'Why can't you view me as a person to be loved rather than a person to be saved?' He replied, 'I don't know you well enough to love you!'"[19]

Is our evangelism just a project whereby we want to get others saved? Or is it based on a love of the other that wants to see him or her experience the fullness, wholeness, joy, and good news that Jesus has to offer?

THINK ABOUT IT
What practices listed above have worked for you in the past?

What strategies would you add to those on the list?

Are there any that are not effective for you or that you hesitate to try? Why?

---

[19]Ibid., 24.

TRY IT OUT
Can any of today's strategies be used as you reach out to persons you know? Select a strategy you will try and, if possible, make contact with them today.

Person	_Strategy_	_Contact Made_
1.		
2.		
3.		

Remember to keep each of these persons in your personal daily prayers.

DAY FIVE: _Inviting a Response_

The good news of Jesus Christ is a message that calls for a response. Of course, not every presentation of the good news will allow for a response. Sometimes, it is enough just to tell your story, or to make mention of how the gospel might intersect with a person's life and situation. Simply telling the good news is appropriate and is often all we are able to accomplish at a particular time.

However, there are times and occasions when it is appropriate to invite a response. Indeed, there are times when the message we share would not be complete without allowing for and inviting the other to respond.

Sometimes, that response will be appropriate only after there have been a number of opportunities to share the good news with a particular person. Other times, the opportunity for response may present itself on the first encounter.

It is important that when we are sharing good news we pray for God's leading in inviting a response. Seek the Holy Spirit's guidance on the timing and kind of response to seek. And remember, inviting a response is not the same as "closing the deal." You do not share the good news with your eye on the bottom line waiting for the other person to make the opening that will allow you to get him to make a response. Your goal is not to collect another scalp for God, but to share good news. Part of sharing good news is to allow the other an opportunity to respond to the good news.

There are different levels of response that can be made. One response might be to invite the person you are with to pray with you. This is especially appropriate if you are sharing with a person who is going through one of life's transition times. After talking with him or her, listening, and sharing a bit of good news, it might be appropriate to offer to pray. The prayer can be simple and brief. Simply ask God to be with the person and to surround him

95

or her with his love and grace. Such a prayer can be offered quietly and gracefully. Most persons will appreciate it and your good news will have made a lasting impression on them.

Sometimes the response that is called for is actually to make a commitment to Jesus Christ. A person who has been seeking and who has heard several presentations of the good news may indicate an interest and a readiness to commit his or her life to Jesus Christ. If you have shared with a person and sense that there is an interest in making such a commitment, offer this person the opportunity to commit his or her life to Christ. A simple prayer of commitment is an appropriate way to allow this response.

Other ways to invite response include inviting the other person to ask questions. This indicates your willingness to go the next step and clarify areas where he or she is still seeking or is still unclear.

THINK ABOUT IT
People can be invited to respond to the good news in any number of ways. We have mentioned prayer as one possible response. Other responses might include singing a song, reciting a creed, or writing in a journal. Use this space to list other possible responses that you could offer or invite. Be creative. There is not one right way to respond to God.

-
-
-
-
-

TRY IT OUT
Imagine that you are sitting on a park bench with a friend who is the mother of a small child. The child has been sick and the mother has expressed her fear and uncertainty to you. After listening, you share your belief that Jesus Christ can offer strength in times such as this. You then say, "Could we pray together?" Write a sample of the prayer you might pray with that mother there on that park bench:

You have been talking with a co-worker about Jesus from time to time over recent weeks. One day after work, he asks you to stay for a few minutes. He says he has been intrigued by what you are sharing and would like to be a follower of Jesus himself. What response would you make? Write your response and sample prayer of commitment here:

DAY SIX: *The Next Step*

What happens next? This is an important question.

Imagine that you have taken this business of sharing good news seriously. You have cultivated relationships, you have discussed the building blocks of the gospel, you have listened, and you have asked invitational questions. You have prayed, and you have invited others to respond. Much to your surprise, those you have been sharing with have responded positively. Several have asked for more information and have opened a dialogue about Jesus Christ and the abundant life he offers. Several persons going through difficult times have discovered in you a sensitive friend and are coming to trust in God to help them through. One or two persons have even asked you to lead them in actually committing their lives to Jesus Christ.

What happens next?

The work of evangelism goes hand in hand with the work of discipleship. Discipleship involves embarking on a life in the community of faith. It includes growing in faith through acts of compassion, justice, worship, and devotion. (See the introduction for more information about these aspects of discipleship.) Discipleship includes growing in Jesus Christ and becoming more and more like him through the process we call sanctification.

THINK ABOUT IT

It is hardly fair to share the gospel, receive a response, and then leave a person on his or her own to live as a disciple. Your responsibility of sharing good news does not end when one has made a commitment to Jesus. Use the "Think About It" section of today's session to brainstorm ways to assist a new or renewed believer on the road to discipleship. Be creative. List as many possibilities as you can come up with. I have even given you a start on your list.

- Begin a Bible Study in your home
- Give your friend a Bible
- Meet together at lunch for a time of prayer
-
-
-
-
-

TRY IT OUT
Is there something on your list that you can begin to do with a person who is responding to your witness?

DAY SEVEN: *Your Next Step*

What is the next step for you?

We have covered a lot of territory these past few weeks. We began with, perhaps, a little uncertainty about talking about Jesus and sharing the good news. I hope that you completed these six weeks with new knowledge, new confidence, and new energy for sharing good news.

Today I invite you to consider where you have come and to make a commitment for where you are going to go. Don't just take this experience and let it gather dust on a shelf or in your mind. Go from here ready to share the good news on a daily basis. Cultivate relationships, stay current on the basic essentials of the gospel, and continue to review and update your own story.

There is an excitement that comes as we tell the story of Jesus. Satisfaction comes in the act of sharing the good news. It also comes because we know we are doing the will of him who calls his disciples to take his message to the ends of the earth.

THINK ABOUT IT
How have you changed or grown during the course of this study?

When you began, you expressed certain hesitations and reservations when it comes to sharing the good news. Which of those do you think you have started to overcome?

Which of those are still obstacles to you?

What has been the most helpful, practical aspect of this study?

TRY IT OUT

What is your plan of action for sharing the good news in the future? Pray about this and list several goals you will work on in the future.

-
-
-
-

What has your experience with this group been like? Where do you see your group going from here?

GROUP MEETING FOR WEEK 5

Praying together

Review of this week's material

Exercises, role plays, or case studies
Divide into pairs. Choose one person to be the sharer of good news and one to be the hearer of the good news. Develop a scenario in which the evangelist invites the hearer to make a response to the good news that has been shared. Share your scenario with the group.

Remain in pairs, switch roles, and devise a new scenario. This allows each partner to have an opportunity to practice inviting a response.

Telling our story

Share together in Holy Communion

Closing prayer time

Discuss the future of this particular group. Where do you go from here?

Evaluation

WORKS CITED

Bales, Harold K. <u>Leading Persons To Christ.</u> Kingsport, Tennessee: Precept, 1992.

Braaten, Carl E. <u>No Other Gospel!</u> Minneapolis: Augsburg Fortress, 1992.

Donaho, Joe. <u>Good News Travels Faster.</u> Decatur, Georgia: CTS Press, 1990.

Fox, H. Eddie, and George E. Morris. <u>Faith Sharing.</u> Nashville: Discipleship Resources, 1986.

Hunter, George G. III. <u>Contagious Congregations</u>. Nashville: Abingdon, 1979.

Knutson, Gerhard. <u>Ministry to Inactives</u>. Minneapolis: Augsburg, 1979.

Outler, Albert C. <u>Evangelism in the Wesleyan Spirit</u>. Nashville: Tidings, 1971.

Outler Albert C., ed. <u>John Wesley</u>. New York: Oxford University Press, 1964.

Pippert, Rebecca Manley. <u>Out of the Saltshaker & Into the World</u>. Downer's Grove, Illinois: Intervarsity, 1979.

THE BUILDING BLOCKS OF THE GOSPEL

A Good God Created a Good Creation
Humans Sin; Creation Is Broken
Jesus of Nazareth
Jesus Dies on a Cross
Jesus Was Raised on the Third Day
God's Kingdom Is Coming
The Good News Calls for a Response

Cut out and carry in your wallet or purse:

THE BUILDING BLOCKS OF THE GOSPEL

A Good God Created a Good Creation
Humans Sin; Creation Is Broken
Jesus of Nazareth
Jesus Dies on a Cross
Jesus Was Raised on the Third Day
God's Kingdom Is Coming
The Good News Calls for a Response